T0339406

# Information Science as an Interscience

# Information Science as an Interscience

## Rethinking Science, Method and Practice

*Carel Stephanus de Beer*

ELSEVIER

AMSTERDAM • BOSTON • HEIDELBERG • LONDON
NEW YORK • OXFORD • PARIS • SAN DIEGO
SAN FRANCISCO • SINGAPORE • SYDNEY • TOKYO

Chandos Publishing is an imprint of Elsevier

CP
CHANDOS
PUBLISHING

Chandos Publishing is an imprint of Elsevier
225 Wyman Street, Waltham, MA 02451, USA
Langford Lane, Kidlington, OX5 1GB, UK

**Notices**
Knowledge and best practice in this field are constantly changing. As new research and experience broaden our understanding, changes in research methods, professional practices, or medical treatment may become necessary.

Practitioners and researchers must always rely on their own experience and knowledge in evaluating and using any information, methods, compounds, or experiments described herein. In using such information or methods they should be mindful of their own safety and the safety of others, including parties for whom they have a professional responsibility.

To the fullest extent of the law, neither the Publisher nor the authors, contributors, or editors, assume any liability for any injury and/or damage to persons or property as a matter of products liability, negligence or otherwise, or from any use or operation of any methods, products, instructions, or ideas contained in the material herein.

ISBN: 978-0-08-100140-0

**British Library Cataloguing-in-Publication Data**
A catalogue record for this book is available from the British Library

**Library of Congress Cataloging-in-Publication Data**
A catalog record for this book is available from the Library of Congress

Library of Congress Control Number: 2015932040

For information on all Chandos Publishing publications
visit our website at http://store.elsevier.com/

Working together
to grow libraries in
developing countries

www.elsevier.com • www.bookaid.org

# Contents

# About the author

**Carel Stephanus de Beer** is Emeritus Professor at the Department of Information Science, University of South Africa (Unisa), Pretoria, South Africa, and is currently an Extraordinary Professor of Information Science at the University of Pretoria. He graduated in Agriculture and Philosophy (doctoral studies) at the University of Pretoria and the University of Paris X, Nanterre, France. He has taught Philosophy, Communications and Information Science at various universities, undertaken research in all these areas, and was involved in consultancy work in the fields of knowledge generation, invention, dissemination and application. His research interests include the philosophy and theory of information, philosophies and theories of technics and technology, and knowledge invention, dissemination and utilisation. He is also committed to research on reading theory and on the reinvention of human spirituality and noology.

The author may be contacted at: fanie.debeer@up.ac.za

# Acknowledgements

I wish to pay a special tribute to the following people:

Professor Johan Bekker, retired head of the Department of Library and Information Science, University of South Africa, Pretoria, who initially dared to bring me, as a relative outsider, into the exciting and stimulating field of library and information science and knowledge and information practice so close to my heart.

Professor Theo Bothma, currently head of the Department of Information Science at the University of Pretoria, who kept me involved in this fascinating field. This happened at a time when I thought my time was over. His inspiring confidence remains a source of great joy and thankfulness. He never left a stone untouched to encourage and support all my intellectual efforts to participate in conferences and research programmes locally and internationally, especially in Paris, France. Professor Bothma remains firmly convinced of the significance of the contributions I am trying to make in the Department, the University, and the field of information science and practice, and even science in general. This generates great enthusiasm in me.

Professor Roelf Sandenberg, the Dean of the Faculty of Engineering, the Built Environment and Information Technology (EBIT) at the University of Pretoria, who never hesitated in a spirit of congeniality to approve my appointments, to sponsor my initiatives of international conference attendance and to enthusiastically support my research endeavours.

Colleagues and friends with great minds and of an international stature, like the Paul Ricoeur, Jacques Derrida, Jean-Jacques Salomon, Gernot Wersig, Rainer Kuhlen, Peter Ingwersen, Sam Weber, Michel Serres, Edgar Morin, Pierre Lévy, Bernard Stiegler, Catherine Malabou, Bruno Latour and Jean-Pierre Dupuy, without whose inspiring works of great intellectual depth and honesty, and their hospitality, personal conversations and communications over many years, this project would not have been possible − with the provision that any lack in quality and insight would not have been due to any fault on their side.

Members of the Chandos Publishing team, Dr Glyn Jones, George Knott and Harriet Clayton, for their unconditional and professional enthusiasm for the project from its inception and the support and interest they have shown during the process of its development. It is simply a pleasure to work with them.

My dear wife, Ilze Holtzhausen de Beer, not only for her unconditional love, commitment and dedication, and sometimes even sacrifices, but also for her intelligent and very significant and immaculate editorial advice and assistance to a 'second-language' writer.

# Introduction

This book is born from the conviction that there is much more to information science, and by implication to knowledge work and information practice, than what the generally accepted views regarding science and its nature and application possibilities are able to offer. These views are currently and in general still based on the slim positivistic model of scientific exploration, the totally inadequate subject/object relationship on which it concentrates, and the unavoidable methodological implications these foci entail. The conviction is inspired by the work done by many scientists and thinkers about science in general over a long period of time, concerned about the limitations and counterproductive outcomes related to science in the traditional sense of the word. Many information scientists and even information practitioners share this concern as reflected in the substantial amount of work done by them.

In order to give effect to this conviction this publication deals with issues in quite a different way than one most probably would expect from a publication of this nature and focus, namely the concentration on the nature of science, method, knowledge and practices. The strangeness will hopefully become intelligible in the development of the contents and structure of the study. Although this publication is not exhaustive of the ambitious theme and project, especially in view of the rich and productive field which the concern is about, it is at least meant to encourage the rethinking of issues related to information science and information and knowledge work and practice.

The first chapter focuses on the distinct capacity of thought that will enable us to transgress boundaries and open new vistas for information scientific exploration. Acritical thinking is proposed as the distinct strategy of thought as opposed to critical thinking which is believed to be trapped in disciplinary and linear actions, unable to really open new perspectives. This approach forms the necessary condition for rethinking information science along similar lines as the rethinking of science in general, as proposed and articulated by many intellectuals engaged in the scientific endeavour. Chapters 2, 3 and 4 concentrate on this rethinking of science, especially with a view to an interscientific position for information science, why this focus is essential and in what terms it can, and perhaps should, be pursued. This approach is certainly met with serious antagonism which varies, on the one hand, from simple refusal (the easiest option) to, on the other hand, the extreme of intense and even insulting animosity. This negativity is very often inspired by a lack of insight and total ignorance about what is really happening in the world of the sciences and the implications of these developments and happenings for library and information science.

The implication of a new and different conception of science requires different methodological strategies which, at the same time as a new thinking about method, also contributes to the new thinking about science. Chapters 5 and 6 are devoted to the exploration of alternative methodological issues, contrary to the boring generalised and generally accepted approaches to method as manifested in the multitude of methodological handbooks currently on the market. Method needs imagination and ample room should be made for such an imaginative initiative where representative thinking is transcended and manages to go beyond its boundaries and sterilising limitations in order to open up avenues of and for invention.

As can be expected, a new scientific dispensation with new methodological endeavours would require a rethinking of the nature of knowledge and information as well. The effort to articulate such a new knowledge dispensation is pursued in Chapter 7. This newness and freshness in the knowledge approach and dynamics will hopefully enable substantial new qualities of knowledge work and new impacts of knowledge and information on societies in desperate need for solutions to the never-ending endemic problems diverse in nature and intensity. This implies a strong battle for intelligence and an equally fierce battle against ignorance and the vast consequences this entails.

The implication is that the requirements for significant and enlightening knowledge work by knowledge workers will be unique, different from the generally accepted monotonous and sedimented approaches, due to equally dormant scientific approaches, and quite demanding but even more exciting for 'the age of exciting developments' in which we live. Chapter 8 deals with these requirements fairly extensively because, as can be expected, a new dispensation for thinking in an acritical sense, for science in an ambulant mood, for method in noological terms, and knowledge and information with a transformational inspiration in the sense of multiple connective intellection as its focus, will certainly pose exciting but also demanding challenges to the knowledge worker not to be ignored.

This whole endeavour is inspired by a specific ethical sensitivity as articulated in the expression 'science with conscience' for which Morin, Deleuze, Lyotard, Serres, Levinas and many others provide the necessary stimulation and foundation. The unfortunate separation of scientific endeavours from ethical convictions, challenges and demands, as it manifests itself currently in policies and strategies, proves to be fatal from a societal as well as individual perspective, but also from the perspective of the future of the human race. The warnings by many about coming and fatal catastrophes, many of which have already been experienced, may be related to ignorance regarding skewed intellectual foci and developments (distorted, blindfolded, one-sided, reductionistic) that may have barbaric consequences.

Many intellectuals, philosophers, scientists and writers shaped and are still shaping my mind as reflected in these studies. It should, however, be clear from each of these chapters the thankful and appreciative indebtedness in a personal and intellectual capacity to Michel Serres for the inspiration flowing from his work of almost 50 years, from his first publication in 1969 of *La communication* to his very latest of which I am aware, namely *Pantopie* in 2014, and every one of his more than 60 books is related to this theme. They coloured my whole career of involvement in information science and work over more than 25 years. The excitement and joy I experienced during all these years in this field would not have been the same, if at all, without his phenomenal contribution at both a personal and intellectual level.

What is remarkable is that his conception of information represents neither the current culture of informationalism nor information as a mere commodity. For him information is a message and a message not to be absolutised nor put up for sale. Messages have transformative power with respect to the world in which we live, the societies of which we form part, the individuals who we are, and the messengers have a responsibility for the quality of the impact, or lack of it, of the messages they generate.

While my effort is a tribute to his work it does not mean for a single moment that it must be considered as work done on the same level and of the same intensity and depth as his. It is merely an expression of deep gratitude.

As happens with the compilation of a book from previously published articles, often published over a period of time, the different chapters are in a sense independent from each other despite the links that interconnect them and the initial intention to develop them with a view to eventually becoming a book. There may be duplications and overlaps while at the same time a certain development of ideas, thoughts and insights will certainly be detected. The implication is that the different chapters can easily be read separately but reading them as a unity will hopefully make an equal amount of sense.

The further hope is that the exploration of the literature as reflected in the list of references will encourage readers to further explore the wealth and depth of intellectual capacity demonstrated in the literature sometimes discussed in more detail and in other cases only touched upon. Every single text referred to deserves serious attention and may even pose a challenge to be reflected upon in a time and age of growing illiteracy and deliberate ignorance about literature. This may make up for the necessary limitations, shortcomings and incompleteness that can be expected from a publication of this nature on such a vast field. At least the literature may make those involved in information science and information and knowledge work aware of the fact that there are widely published sources by formidable authors on themes such as responsible science, enlightening wisdom and the fulfilment of meaning. These themes may not necessarily be very popular in these circles and not high on their agendas but nevertheless are themes that constitute from another perspective the real focus and decisive factor of the field of information science and practice.

# An acritical philosophy of information

**1**

## 1.1 Introduction

Reflection on knowledge, information, the sciences, philosophy and literature always takes place in a biospheric, technological, economic and cultural environment, from which it draws its resources and on which it will produce its effects. This situation of intellectual activity in a complex and multi-layered environment can be referred to as knowledge ecology. This term refers to the network of relations linking human activity to a natural environment that both constrains it and is altered by it, and by which specific activities such as intellectual interventions or interferences take place in a dynamic, situational relation to socio-cultural contexts.

The production and forms of knowledge or scientific developments and the character and role of cognitive activity have neither existence nor meaning outside their relation to this techno-economico-cultural environment. This contextualisation is itself a form of knowledge, designated in different sites and situations by terms such as ecology, context theory, cybernetic holism, complex adaptive systems or actor-network theory. The project of an acritical philosophy of information is nothing but a defence of the necessity for 'the philosophical' in our cognitive, epistemic and informational endeavours, and simultaneously a manner of refusing the aestheticist, formalist or ideological marginalisation of the philosophical. This underlines the fact that there are many things that the disciplinary discourses do not or cannot know, not even when these discourses accumulate into one huge pile of knowledges.

A further perspective on these domains, sites and situations that lies beyond disciplinary exercises and that calls for another kind of investigation and reflection has been detected by the architect Bernard Tschumi (1998). He emphasises the importance of taking cognisance of the exterior of any discipline and its possible impact on the discipline. Martin Heidegger's appeal for practising 'adequate reflection' links up with the view of Tschumi that there is something outside the generally accepted status of scientific endeavours. Heidegger (1977) refers to this reflection as the courage to turn the truth of our own presuppositions and the realm of our own goals into the things that most deserve to be questioned. Presuppositions, assumptions, prejudices and personal preferences play an immensely important role in what will eventually be considered to be scientific knowledge. Paul Ricœur (1991: 465) emphasises something similar in relation to language and poetry: 'My philosophical project is to show how human language is inventive despite the objective limits and codes which govern it, to reveal the diversity and potentiality of language which the erosion of everyday, conditioned by technocratic and political [and scientific and professional] interests, never ceases to obscure.' He sketches the responsibility of the philosopher as follows: 'to preserve the varieties of the uses of language and the polarities between these different kinds of language, ranging from science through political and practical language and ordinary language, let us say poetry. And ordinary language mediating between poetry, on one hand, and scientific language, on the other hand' (Ricœur, 1991: 448). Here the emphasis is on the dimensions of language that lie outside the disciplinary languages but which most certainly affect these languages.

Hans-Georg Gadamer, using statistics as an example, shows how the hermeneutical dimension encompasses the entire procedure of science. He points out that science always operates in definite conditions of methodological abstraction, and that the successes of modern sciences rest on the fact that other possibilities for questioning are concealed by this abstraction. In the process, truth becomes distorted and even obfuscated. Other facts will come to the fore if other questions are asked, questions he considers to be hermeneutic questions. Other questions might generate other meanings of the facts and other consequences. Here he invites the decisive function of fantasy or imagination to elaborate and connect facts, meanings and consequences (Gadamer, 1976: 11–13).

It should be clear from these few remarks that not only is the philosophical always with us but that there exists a central and fundamentally important place for it. But 'the philosophical', or philosophy, in what sense? There are so many different approaches.

## 1.2  Philosophy as an act of thinking

Philosophy and more specifically 'the philosophical' as a human characteristic or even disposition (and not philosophical schools) is about human thinking and how human thinking finds expression and fulfils an orientation function in many situations. Thinking remains very probably the most special capacity humans possess — all humans. Thinking, in as far as it is a noetic endeavour, teaches us the very art of living (Morin, 2004: 151–9; also see Morin's studies on Ideas, 1991). Morin (1991: 12) writes: 'Our most profound lack is the lack of wisdom.' We need to revisit the idea of wisdom we inherited from the thought of antiquity but have lost in modern times.

'The work of thinking well' Pascal raised includes reflection: self-examination, self-critique that struggles constantly against internal illusions and lying to oneself, as well as the questioning of assumptions, prejudices and personal preferences. At the same time it entails the avoidance of unilateral ideas, mutilated conceptions and views regarding important matters, and the search to conceive of human complexity. The main challenge posed to our unique capacity to think is, then, think well, since this is our highest moral principle!

As such, philosophy is the human effort to delve deep, as deeply as possible, into the spiritual and mental activities of humans in all situations, not only in matters of life but also in matters of science and knowledge, matters of human creativity and inventiveness and human faults, failure and despair. All these activities inspire and motivate humans to act. Never are authentic philosophical investigations, although sometimes very critical, meant to be destructive. They support humans and they support and guide human endeavours such as science, culture and practices.

Philosophy does not take anything for granted. It questions everything in a search for truth and truthfulness. Humans reflect on their lives, their goals, their convictions, their beliefs. Serious reflection does not hesitate to delve deep into the origins and foundations that direct and guide these issues. Humans articulate, that is they put into words what they discover in these processes. In short, they try to give meaning to what they discover. This meaning-giving activity is called conceptualisation. Working with concepts, analysing concepts, organising and reorganising concepts comprise the work or activity of the philosopher or of the philosophical in us.

Philosophy does this in a structured and focused way. Deleuze and Guattari (1994) can help us greatly in this regard. I will briefly return to them at a later stage. No science, no writing, no thinking can happen without concepts. But concepts are relational, they relate all the time to domains other than the domains of their immediate activity. Concepts relate and connect the history of thought, history of science and history of human life. As such, when it is true to its nature, philosophy is much more of a compositional than an oppositional activity (Stiegler, 2003). Its critical function is a secondary and not an original function. It starts with and emerges out of a sense of wonder rather than an enthusiasm for critique and criticism. For Michel Serres, as he expressed it in an interview with Bruno Latour, knowledge has two modes: 'The concern with verification and the burdens it requires, but also risk taking, the production of newness, the multiplicity of found objects — in short, inventiveness. It is better to avoid diminishing the second aspect in favour of the first. Begin with one, continue with the other' (Serres, 1995: 126). This takes us beyond mere criticism.

The project of an acritical philosophy is inspired by Bruno Latour's essay on the philosophy of Michel Serres in which he distinguishes between a 'critique' tradition of philosophy and an acritical philosophy approach while characterising Serres' philosophy as acritical: 'The Enlightenment Without the Critique: A Word on Michel Serres' Philosophy' (Latour, 1987). This should be read together with the very enlightening section on 'The End of Criticism' in the conversations of Serres (1995) with Latour. Being fascinated by Serres' philosophy anyhow, especially in view of his focus on information and knowledge networks and interdisciplinarity, the philosophy of information, which provides an excellent focus for information science as interscience, and furthermore frustrated by philosophies, philosophical systems and the general attitude of the 'critique' tradition that drives them, this acritical disposition and what it entails becomes a tempting project. And for this reason, it also focuses on 'the philosophical' as a fundamental human dispositional entity, instead of 'philosophies' and their ideological obsession with critique and the absolutisation of criticism. Chapter 9 deals with this in much more detail, although with a different focus and context in mind, with the excellent differentiation between the two modes of philosophising as made explicit by Latour and the usefulness of the acritical approach not only as a characterisation of Serres' philosophy, but also as a

philosophical approach generally detectable in the work of various other philosophers and as an exceptionally suitable approach for information science.

In this way philosophy can contribute immensely to the inventive endeavours of
the sciences, especially when it is embraced for what it is worth and if philosophy
itself lives up to its true expectations.

## 1.3  Philosophy and science

Does this general understanding of philosophical activity relate to something such
as a scientific discipline, for example information science? As it delves into the
depths of human reality it delves equally deeply into the depths of scientific reality.
The intriguing phenomenon of paradigms demonstrates exactly how deeply scientific reality is seated and anchored in human reality (see Morin, 1983). We must
never forget that the reality of science is part of human reality. And as such it is
and will always be affected by the depths of this reality. Beliefs, convictions,
assumptions and prejudices that colour our very lives cover the endeavours we are
involved in. Science undeniably forms one of these endeavours.

The surroundings of science, the milieu in which scientific work proceeds, are
equally important. For this reason the ecology of science and of scientific knowledge is similarly of central importance (see Kuhlen, 2004). Ideological, political,
socio-cultural and religious issues play a significant role in the construction of the
sciences. Isabelle Stengers (2000) suggests, for example, that we might interpret the
tension between scientific objectivity and belief as a necessary part of science, central to the practices invented and reinvented by scientists. This takes us far beyond
the 'critique' tradition, the disciplinary tradition, in the direction of the interdisciplinary and the interscientific.

The terminology of science, its vocabulary and its language require philosophical
and conceptual accompaniment. Diverse dimensions of language fall outside the disciplinary discourses but exercise considerable influence on the discourses of science. The
scientist must be careful not to take possession and claim sole proprietorship of terminology and concepts derived from the history of thought as if they are creations of science.
This is highlighted in the work by Sokal and Bricmont (1998) on the use and abuse of
concepts and the debate between Debray and Bricmont (2003) on the same theme.
Human rationality in all its forms and in all its ambiguities forms the basis of the debate.
Another example is the work of Isabelle Stengers (1997). She makes a case for the concept of complexity that transcends the conventional boundaries of scientific discourse,
of the 'critique' tradition, and that clearly exposes the risks of scientific thinking.

## 1.4  Philosophy and information science

The uniqueness of information science does not exempt it from the above remarks.
In fact it reinforces the above in relation to the informational context and milieu and
therefore calls for a unique kind of philosophical approach and input. If information

science is understood as an interscience (see Chapter 2), then the suggestions by Gernot Wersig (1992, 1993) about the role of interconcepts makes a good deal of sense and needs to be carefully explored. The new situation of knowledge as elaborated by him also requires a new type of science. Information science is not to be looked at as a classical discipline, but as a prototype of this new kind of science (see Chapters 2 to 4). It stands to reason that this calls for a new kind of thinking, because knowledge, science and thinking are always interdependent. It is here that his suggestions about 'interconcepts' and the 'weaver-bird approach' of knitting concepts, insights, terms and fragments of information together into sensible entities are relevant. Examples of such interconcepts are knowledge, image, technology, culture, reality and ideas. 'They are concepts of strong self-evidence, of an apparent familiarity, they penetrate a lot of disciplines and common discourses, but themselves do not have a scientific domicile' (Wersig, 1993: 234). They are used everywhere without a clear understanding of them in all their manifestations and embodiments. There is a need for these interconcepts to be rethought and reformulated in order to reach a new understanding of them in terms of their origins and comprehensive manifestations. Obviously such an initiative calls for a philosophical approach of a certain kind and opens the way to an interscientific conception of information science.

Bougnoux (1993), in his consideration of philosophical approaches and their value for information science and practice, draws our attention to a number of important issues that should be thoroughly explored for relevance for an acritical approach:

- *The origins of human reason.* Is reason innate or a product of exchanges and the sum of arguments? To be reasonable is to be nothing else but engaged in communication. No human competence can actualise itself outside the context of discursive activities. This inevitably leads to pragmatics (Bougnoux, 1993: 22).
- *Pragmatics.* In affirming the primacy of relations, pragmatics tends to further undermine the transcendence or innateness of reason. Peirce affirms this and in this affirmation underlines one of the major issues of Popper's epistemology. Latour emphasises that there is nothing in the scientific initiative that opposes in any essential way the incentives of politics. Scientific activity contains a kind of moral obligation: opening or communication. To be reasonable means dialogue in a decentred space, anarchistic in the strong sense.
- *Writing.* Human reason is partly related to its utensils or tools of which writing is the first, and writing should be related to another very crucial term: logocentrism. Logocentrism refers to the pretensions of logos (at the same time reason, language and calculation) to be central to human intellectual endeavours. Logocentrism mistrusts all mediations and dreams of immediacy, or of presence to the self of subjects in all domains. At the same time it constitutes the cornerstone of a critical approach, an approach which is questioned in this article. The question of writing is one of technics, and the question of technics remains central to our studies, albeit with another kind of focus than that of technicism.
- *Imagination.* In opposition to reason, imagination remains a matter of real concern for philosophers. Imagination cannot be eliminated from the heart of human intellectual endeavours. There are simply too many things or matters that reason and rationality in the strict sense cannot really account for. The free circulation of information becomes important here and should be related to the activity of imaginative informatisation (see De Beer, 1992, 2000).

- *The general connection between disciplines.* Among the numerous themes that are of interest to both information science and philosophy is this theme of the general interconnectedness of disciplines, which actually means the general connection between knowledges. Note, for instance, the previous remarks on interconcepts that establish a straightforward connection. Our knowledges run in circles and strengthen one another all the time. A solidarity exists between knowledges. But they can also interfere strongly in one another's affairs.
- *What is science for?* Its purpose and goal fall outside the strictly scientific field when science is understood as the investigation of a certain object or objects by means of, or with the help of, specific appropriate methods. The method and object of physics, for example, falls outside the domain of questions about what physics may be for and what can be done with it.

These are all philosophical issues pertaining to information science in a special way, later re-emphasised by Bougnoux (1998). In view of these non-scientific, more specifically philosophical issues, which are always present in our deliberations of what science is, it is remarkable how many people disregard philosophy as if it is not the most important thing in our lives and with how much ease this is done. Aristotle, the great Greek philosopher, was very explicit about this: either one should philosophise or one should not philosophise, but if one should not philosophise then this can happen only in the name of philosophy. Nothing is more amusing than the tactics of the supposed enemies of philosophy who introduce grandiose philosophical arguments in order to show that there is no philosophy.

## 1.5   Modes of thinking

These modes of thinking will take us beyond the 'critique' tradition. Among the greatest enemies of the philosophical endeavour is the diversity of trends and schools of philosophy and the animosity between them. The presence of philosophical activity in the sciences often reflects a kind of sympathy for one school or another. What the different schools have in common is at least the shared enthusiasm for thinking as a human activity. This is probably the most significant aspect of philosophy and can be applied everywhere. The pursuit of thinking, rather than a specific philosophical trend, aims to avoid domination by any specific school. It wants to profit from the energies of human thought that are released from the diverse schools. The focus would then be rather on thought itself and how it should be applied than on schools or trends.

We should opt for a mode or modes of thinking that will be able to respond constructively to the interscientific, polymorphic, multi-faceted nature of information science and its engagements. There are many different ways in which we can explain thinking, some more adequate than others. The kind of emphasis we put on thinking will determine the direction thinking is going to take regarding many issues, such as knowledge, method, science and ethics. There will be vast implications for fields such as knowledge management (functionalistic or complexity driven), research methods (qualitative and quantitative, but also the notion of a method that will accommodate what cannot be classified under quality and quantity), the character of science as a strictly objectifying activity or of science as a dynamic process which takes account of both necessity and chance, of both crystalline hardness and smoky suppleness and subtlety, and of ethics in terms of inner conviction and interhuman engagement, rather than numerous lists of powerless ethical codes with which people have to comply.

In order to comply with the description of information science as an interscience (see Chapter 2), I wish to explore a possible approach to thinking that will facilitate this science. Certainly the sciences need their facilitators, especially in terms of the philosophical. Most of the time they do it themselves: Atlan, Prigogine, Ekeland, Heisenberg and many others. It is my conviction that thinking, understood in terms of the critical/acritical debate, the multi-faceted nature of information, the complex nature of these issues in general, and the challenge to invent alternatives for oneself as well as for communities, lead us to describe appropriate thinking as acritical in the following terms: this mode of thinking is or should be complex, multiple and inventive.

These terms are irreductionistic or anti-reductionistic. They will enable us to get a sensible and honest picture of the relevance of thinking and of relevant thinking of a special kind at the heart of information science as a special kind of science, and they will be carefully explored.

The suggestions of Bernard Stiegler (2003) serve as a point of departure for this exploration when he emphasises the importance of thinking in compositional and not oppositional terms. Oppositional thinking is typical of critical thinking and is characterised by exclusion, rejection, comparison and linearity. Although this mode of thinking is well-established, is useful in many respects and fulfils important functions, it remains inadequate when it comes to the fullness and comprehensiveness of reality and knowledges about reality. A way to cope with this is to think in compositional terms. Built into the capacity of compositional thinking is the ability to find something different, unexpected and new. This is what mostly happens in scientific inventions (Stengers, 1997, 2000).

There is a world of difference between an acritical approach to thinking and a critical approach, a difference which extends to the outcomes of their practical applications. The first is fertile and productive and the second sterile, repetitive and counterproductive. The one is inspirational and the other debilitating.

Michel Serres is probably, in the context of information philosophy, the most important exponent of the acritical approach (see previous reference to the acritical approach). His Hermes series of five volumes provides ample demonstration and illustration of this, explicitly merely from his exegesis of the terms he uses for this purpose: communication, distribution, transference, translation, the north-west passage (interdisciplinary passages between the sciences). None of these terms can really be confined to the boundaries of a critical approach. With the help of each, Michel Serres invites us to share with him his journeys into the dynamic and open spaces of knowledges and information developments (see De Beer, 1990, for an elaboration of these terms).

Acritical thinking manifests itself or is characterised by the following modes of thinking: the notion of complexity, multiplicity and inventiveness. These modes of thinking are strongly suggested by the acritical approach of Michel Serres.

### 1.5.1 Complex thinking

Complex thinking as discussed by Morin (1990a: 15−24) is more than adequate, and the way he relates this to information and knowledge is highly significant. In a discussion of blind intelligence Morin emphasises that error, ignorance and blindness progress simultaneously with our knowledges. We have to take radical cognisance of developments in this regard. The profound cause of error does not lie in factual errors (false perceptions) or in logical errors (incoherence) but in the way in which knowledge is organised into systems of ideas (theories and ideologies) without our recognising and apprehending the complexity of the real. What is inevitably created is a one-dimensional vision that leads to the pathology of knowledge and blind intelligence.

Our disjunctions, abstractions and reductions create 'a paradigm of simplification'. Such a strategy eliminates the philosophical and in this process prohibits those in the sciences from exercising self-knowledge, self-reflection and even the ability to conceive of themselves scientifically. The inevitable consequence is an effort to simplify the complex as well. Measurement and calculation are the only things that count. Simplified thinking is unable to see the connection between the one and the multiple and diversity is thereby destroyed. The consequence: blind intelligence. Blind intelligence destroys totalities and togetherness; it isolates all objects from their milieu and environment. A new, massive and productive ignorance is created, together with an inability to conceive complexity, hence the challenge to contemplate the necessity for complex thinking.

What is complexity? In the first place it is like a tissue, binding together heterogeneous constituent issues. It is, in effect, a tissue of the events, actions, interactions, retroactions, determinations and risks which together constitute our world. But then the notion of complexity confronts us with the mad, the disorderly, the ambiguous and the uncertain. The challenge to thinking is to continuously link the simple and the complex in order to avoid and eliminate the sickness of inadequate dogmatistic theories, the pathology of reason manifested in a partial, unilateral system of ideas that does not acknowledge that part of reality is irrational and not measurable, that rationality has to enter into constant dialogue with the irrational instead of denying it and wishing it away. Thinking of this order can be considered to be complex thinking. (See also Morin (1990b: 304−9) for the commandments of complexity.)

### 1.5.2 Multiple thinking

This and no other kind of thinking can really comply with the dynamic and multi-faceted character of information. Deleuze and Guattari (1994) demonstrate this in a unique way in their discussions of the works of Marcel Proust and Friedrich Nietzsche and the notion of representation. According to them, binary logic and bi-univocal relations still dominate psychoanalysis (see the tree of delirium in Freud), linguistics and structuralism, and even information theory. This domination certainly also covers the field of knowledge in terms of the tree of knowledge. Binary logic is the intellectual reality of the root-tree and must be linked to classical thought, which requires a strong principal unity that includes the linear unity of the word, or even of language. The language of Joyce, with its multiple roots, in effect shatters the linear unity of the word. Nietzsche's aphorisms shatter the linear unity of knowledge.

This limited binary thought has never understood multiplicity. In the domain of multiplicity the principles of connection and heterogeneity rule. The image of the rhizome is used: any point on a rhizome can be connected with any other and may lead to disorder or chaos (see Deleuze and Guattari, 1983). This is very different from the image of the tree or root, which fixes a point and thus an order and confines us to a sphere of discourse that still implies modes of arrangement and particular social types of power. A rhizome never ceases to connect semiotic chains, organisations of power and events in the arts, sciences and social struggles. This keenness to connect characterises the multiple or multiplicity. The implications for knowledges are self-evident and dramatic. A strategy of multiple thinking must be cultivated in order to comply with the challenges of the multiple and to respond to them by processes of connecting and combination. Out of the connections and combinations emerges the new. Inventions become a reality (Serres, 1997).

### 1.5.3 Inventive thinking

This mode of thinking is arguably the culmination of the fruitful encounter between human thinking and knowledge for action, which is information. Bernard Tschumi (1998), in his characterisation of inventive thinking, fixes our attention on the enormous possibilities of the combination, in so many unexpected ways, of issues that are not in an obvious way connectable and demonstrates how new knowledges can emerge from this. He encourages cultural inventions. His architectural plans show the structures of relations that produce inventions. This certainly includes human relations. Inventions tend to occur when unrelated areas, ideas and forms come together in unexpected ways. This entails the dislocation of conventions by using concepts from diverse discursive fields that connect any particular field with its outside. He deliberately subverts the coherence and self-assured stability of a composition and promotes instability and programmatic madness, since madness and meaning together constitute, according to him, inventive possibilities.

## 1.6 Conclusion

Attention should be given to the fruitful ways in which computer developments do facilitate precisely these different kinds of thinking, although this discussion has no room for such attention. The contribution of Pierre Lévy (1993) in this regard with his emphasis on technologies of intelligence is particularly significant. He elaborates the idea of the future of human thinking in the information age, or the age of technologies of intelligence, which would contribute significantly to the idea of an acritical approach in information science as well as the development of the idea of information science as an interscience, the theme of the next chapter.

# References

Bougnoux, D. (1993). *Sciences de l'information et de la communication.* Paris: Larousse.

Bougnoux, D. (1998). *Introduction aux sciences de la communication.* Paris: La Decouverte.

De Beer, C. S. (1990). Hermes overtaken? In *Pitfalls in the Research Process.* Pretoria: HSRC.

De Beer, C. S. (1992). Informatization of society: social engineering or social responsibility. *South African Journal for Library and Information Science, 60*(1), 1−7.

De Beer, C. S. (2000). Societal informatization: the exploration of an idea. *Mousaion, 18*(1), 72−79.

Debray, R., & Bricmont, J. (2003). *A l'ombre des Lumières: debat entre un philosophe et un scientifique.* Paris: Odile Jacob.

Deleuze, G., & Guattari, F. (1983). *On the line.* New York: Semiotext(e).

Deleuze, G., & Guattari, F. (1994). *What is philosophy?* London: Verso.

Gadamer, H.-G. (1976). *Philosophical hermeneutics.* Berkeley, CA: University of California Press.

Heidegger, M. (1977). The age of the world picture. In *The question concerning technology, and other essays.* New York: Garland.

Kuhlen, R. (2004). *Informationsethik: umgang mit wissen und information in elektronischen Raumen.* Konstanz: UVK Verlagsgesellschaft.

Latour, B. (1987). The enlightenment without the critique: a word on Michel Serres' philosophy. In A. Phillips Griffiths (Ed.), *Contemporary french philosophy.* Cambridge: Cambridge University Press.

Lévy, P. (1993). *Les technologies de l'intelligence: l'avenir de la pensée à l'ère informatique.* Paris: La Découverte.

Morin, E. (1983). Social paradigms of scientific knowledge. *SubStance, 39,* 3−20.

Morin, E. (1990a). *Introduction à la pensée complexe.* Paris: ÉSF Éditeur.

Morin, E. (1990b). *Science avec conscience.* Paris: Seuil.

Morin, E. (1991). *La méthode 4. Les idées: leur habitat, leur vie, leurs mœurs, leur organisation.* Paris: Seuil.

Morin, E. (2004). *La méthode 6: Éthique.* Paris: Seuil.

Ricœur, P. (1991). The creativity of language. In Mario J. Valdés (Ed.), *A ricœur reader: reflection and imagination.* Toronto: University of Toronto Press.

Serres, M. (1995). *Conversations on science, culture, and time.* Ann Arbor, MI: University of Michigan Press.

Serres, M. (1997). *The troubadour of knowledge.* Ann Arbor, MI: University of Michigan Press.

Sokal, A., & Bricmont, J. (1998). *Intellectual impostures.* London: Profile Books.

Stengers, I. (1997). *Power and invention.* Minneapolis, MN: Minnesota University Press.

Stengers, I. (2000). *The invention of modern science.* Minneapolis, MN: University of Minneapolis Press.

Stiegler, B. (2003). *Aimer, s'aimer, nous aimer.* Paris: Galilée.

Tschumi, B. (1998). *Architecture and disjunction.* Cambridge, MA: MIT Press.

Wersig, G. (1992). Information science and theory: a weaver bird's perspective. In P. Vakkari, & B. Cronin (Eds.), *Conceptions of library and information science.* London: Taylor Graham.

Wersig, G. (1993). Information science: the study of postmodern knowledge usage. *Information Processing and Management, 29*(2), 229−239.

# Towards the idea of information science as an interscience

2

## 2.1  Introduction

Much has been written about information science as a science and a number of important authors have made valid and valuable points (e.g. Belkin, 1978; Ingwersen, 1995; Kochen, 1983; Saracevic, 1999; Vakkari, 1994; Vakkari & Cronin, 1992; Wersig, 1993a, 1993b). No one has come up with a final viewpoint acceptable to all. This is, however, the case with all sciences – in fact it is true of science in general. New points are constantly raised, all from different perspectives. New developments encourage and allow us to take a new and fresh look at things.

New developments can instil fear, which explains why people are inclined to stick to things they know and consider valuable, or of ultimate importance, or as coming from the right perspective, or as the best way of looking at things, and so forth. In sticking to the familiar they ensure some security at least. On the other hand, this approach can easily lead to stagnation, intellectual starvation, boredom and monotony. That is why debate is important and will always be important. Debate gives rise to new and different, sometimes even unacceptable, views that must be considered and reconsidered.

The purpose of this contribution is to emphasise the core aspect of the scientific endeavour which is currently largely neglected, or at least miniaturised, owing to the sole focus on research and research methods. What has been forgotten is that reflection, namely the intellectual activity in science, is fundamental to science, including information science. Indeed, it is ever present and active, although most of the time it is hidden and not articulated in research methods. What method to choose, how to apply the chosen method, and what to infer from its findings are all reflective, or intellectual, activities.

This contribution therefore focuses on the challenges some contemporary situations and developments pose to the intellectual activities of the scientific endeavour. The assumption is that science is first and foremost an intellectual activity, and the term 'intellectual' is understood in a way closely related to its etymological sense. In other words, it reflects the ultimate in human rational and thinking ability, the ability to read between the lines and to establish links in a comprehensive sense. The question then will be: how do we, as information scientists, respond intellectually to what is happening in the world, especially in our world of information and knowledge development and work, given the context set by current events? It seems as though drastically new socio-cultural and knowledge landscapes are in the process of being constructed.

## 2.2    Changes in landscape

A double change in this landscape poses dramatic challenges to human intellectual activities, which include, of course, scientific intellectual activities.

In the first place, under the impact of developments in the field of electronic media, and information and communication technologies (ICTs) in particular, there has been a radical change in the socio-cultural landscape. Globalisation, which no one can escape any longer, is a good example of this change that opened up our boundaries. This process is comprehensive and leaves almost nothing untouched. Bougnoux (1993: 9–19) gives a number of telling examples: the rapid extension in the Western world of information apparatuses; the decline of the religious; the decline of the rural world; the extension of the markets; the penetration of production by information; the decline of war and the growing ideology of dialogue; the emergence of an ecological conscience; and the division of the labour of knowledge that divides the culture which was, until recently, structured in terms of the humanities, the sciences and mass media.

These three cultures ignore and even scorn each other. The idea of an encyclopaedia, and the possibility of encyclopaedic connections between the three, make people laugh. Nevertheless, periodically, several voices emerge accusing these mutilated knowledges of producing barbarisms (Steiner, 1999). Here the themes and problems of the information sciences have a role to play, and our discipline, following the example of philosophy, could propose some useful links to combat imprisonment. This opening is also somehow a turn. Information is not an object, the contents of which one can simply calculate, as many would claim. It cannot be limited to a place. It establishes links, and maintains itself in the 'inter' of the media and the disciplines – the process of informatisation.

What globalisation signifies is the transgression of boundaries, in other words the opening up of new comprehensive territories to be explored. What must be emphasised is the role and place of ICTs in this regard. This impact is fairly dramatic, but note that these developments should not be viewed as deterministic. In the process, dogmatisms, reductionisms, culturalisms and ideologies that usually set boundaries and close up domains become relativised and are sometimes rejected and even fall away.

Another change involves the contemporary knowledge landscape. Over a number of decades, a new knowledge dispensation, in terms of which knowledge is understood and articulated differently from that described before, has emerged (De Beer, 1996, 2001, 2003). The notion of a 'rhizome' developed by Deleuze and Guattari (1987) and the 'network idea' of Latour (1987) and Callon (1989) which developed into the 'actor-network theory' as inspired by the work of Michel Serres, are both efforts to articulate these developments in the complex field of knowledge and information. The idea of thinking of knowledge in terms of knowledge networks has gradually been established (Parrochia, 2001; Serres, 1994).

Knowledge can no longer be understood as something fixed and final, as something that can rigidly be determined. Knowledge is dynamic, flexible, living and liberating and capable of being opened up to new avenues, perspectives and futures. The intriguing question of the relationship between knowledge and information emerges time and again. The relationship is certainly influenced by and should find new dimensions in these terms. It has not been settled by anyone despite numerous efforts of a more or less epistemological nature. This relationship still needs further exploration. The effort by Stiegler (2010) at least saves the real meaning of knowledge and articulates the current understanding of information quite well, especially in view of 'the idea of the culture of informationalism' of Manuel Castells. Stiegler (2010: 110) explains:

> *Understanding ... appeared only with the advent of writing, which constructed its object as a* knowable *object, stripped of mystery. But the object of understanding, of knowledge, can never fully be reduced to this construction: there is an irreducible inadequacy between knowledge and its object; this inadequacy or incompleteness is inscribed in the very heart of the individuation process that is based on a conception of understanding as* desiring *its object: the object of knowledge is infinite because it is the object of desire. Plato and Aristotle declare that knowledge is not reducible to a technique, a* simple mode of production *of its object, since the object of knowledge ... is also the object of love and desire. It is object-as-affect. The true, the just, and the beautiful have an effect on me, transcending my understanding as such: they transform me. This intrinsic transcendence of the understanding by its object is what requires the individuation of 'the one who knows' by* what *he knows (its object), where the knower is transformed ...*

This is exactly what one may call the process of informatisation.

Added to this Stiegler emphasises that 'while teaching institutions are crumbling and a systematic symbolic misery reigns instead' the consequence is

> *a psychological and social disaster whose overriding consequence is the liquidation of our cognitive faculty itself, and its replacement by information dexterity. The cognitive faculty − what we call reason − is the only solid link between the psychic and the social in that it is passed through the succession of generations transformed and sublimated by disciplinary learning; this process constitutes knowledge. Informational saturation, on the other hand, desocializes the consumer of that information. Knowledge and understanding must be psychically assimilated and made one's own (one's own self), while information is merchandise made to be consumed − and is therefore 'disposable'. (2010: 183−4)*

This understanding of information, which is in line with the general contemporary understanding in terms of 'the culture of informationalism' cancels the dream of informatisation, unless it can be revised and brought closer to knowledge.

The suggestion here is that attention be given to the views of Kuhlen (1990), who writes that 'information is knowledge in action', and Wersig (1993a), who supported and shared Kuhlen's views on this. Both of them accept that information is knowledge for action. Knowledge should be transformed into something workable and applicable that is called information. I think this view frees us from stagnation. This brings information closer to knowledge which is certainly more fruitful from the point of view of information and knowledge work, and of course the process of informatisation.

When Lévy (1993: 165–8) articulates the nature of 'cognitive ecology', with specific reference to the impact of the electronic media on our encounters with knowledge (which cannot be ignored), he emphasises that, in a very fundamental way, the knowledge boundaries have shifted or even opened up. He emphasises and highlights a number of significant openings and these views deserve serious attention. The two most important opening principles are the following: one principle states that an intellectual technology must analyse itself as a multiplicity that is indefinitely open − 'the principle of branched multiplicity'; the other emphasises that the sense of a technique or technical development is never given at its conception, nor at any particular moment of its existence, but that it is a matter of contradictory and contingent interpretations of social actors − 'the principle of interpretation'.

## 2.3   Rethinking human thinking

These changes and emphases put high claims on human thinking. In the last analysis, this thinking is our unique human ability, an ability that enables us to cope with the world in which we live. The less developed this ability, the less able we are to cope with our circumstances and challenges. There is, in other words, a call for a new and different way of thinking, not a way of thinking foreign to humans, but a way of thinking shamelessly neglected by humans (see Chapter 1). This mode of thinking is the comprehensive thinking inspired by values rather than reason and truth, a noological thinking that takes humans far beyond the rational and rationalistic mode of thinking. At the same time it must be understood, especially at present, that human thinking is not merely the activity of a solitary and independent individual, even when understood in the noological sense. Certainly it is human persons who think, but only because a mega-cosmopolitical network thinks 'in' them (Lévy, 1993: 196).

It is an immense, extremely complicated network that thinks in multiple ways and in which heterogeneous parties participate. The actors of this network never stop translating, repeating, cutting and inflecting in all senses of the word what they receive from others ... When we stop accepting the individual consciousness as the centre, we will discover a new cognitive landscape that is richer and more complex. The role of these interfaces and connections in the widest sense acquires a capital importance. It really implies the rethinking of our image of the human person.

When this re-emphasis and recontextualisation of human thinking, according to a newly described image of the human person, is neglected, this is very much to our detriment. Lévy writes:

> *Either we cross a new threshold, enter a new stage of hominization, by inventing*
> *some human attribute that is as essential as language but that operates at a much*
> *higher level, or we continue to communicate through the media and think within*

*the context of separate institutions, which contribute to the suffocation and division of intelligence ... But if we are committed to the process of collective intelligence, we will gradually create the technologies, sign systems, forms of social organization and regulation that will enable us to think as a group, concentrate our intellectual and spiritual forces, and negotiate practical real-time solutions to the complex problems we must inevitably confront. (1997: xxvi–xxvii)*

How and where can this comprehensive and value-driven thinking be accommodated, promoted and accomplished? As Castoriades writes:

*To think is not to get out of the cave; it is not to replace the uncertainty of shadows by the clear-cut outlines of things themselves ... To think is to enter the Labyrinth; more exactly, it is to make be and appear a Labyrinth ... It is to lose oneself amidst galleries which exist only because we never tire of digging them; to turn round and round ... until inexplicably this spinning round opens up in the surrounding walls cracks which offer passage. (1984: ix–x)*

The accomplishment of such thinking is probably yet to be discovered, at least in the milieu of what has been referred to as the new knowledge dispensation. This new knowledge dispensation emerged from the reflecting activities of the sciences and philosophies committed to knowledge and to the scientific endeavour. It is self-evident that these changes will influence scientific approaches and approaches to science.

## 2.4   A new scientific approach

A new knowledge dispensation in a new milieu not only goes hand in hand with a new scientific approach but has, to some extent, also been created by this new approach. Momentum is gained for this renewal by the effective workings of the new media (as will become clear later on).

The notion of a 'new scientific spirit', developed and promoted by Bachelard in 1985, immediately comes to mind. Bachelard investigated the ways in which traditional modes of thinking, both within and outside the sciences, have been radically transformed by what he called the 'new scientific spirit'. What is at stake in the struggle between traditional modes of thought and the increasing number of intellectual practices that can no longer easily be assimilated into that tradition or comprehended by it, is nothing less than the idea and ideal of knowledge based on a notion of truth conceived in terms of 'correspondence' (*adequation intellectus et rei*). The adequation conception of truth presupposes both the separation of thought from its object and the priority of the latter over the former. It is this separation or distinction that the operations of the new scientific spirit have rendered problematic. The notion of intellectual and scientific autonomy is increasingly being questioned today – a tradition that still dominates vast areas of academic activity and academic institutions. This notion presupposes a field that is self-contained and subject to its own laws, principles and rules that are, in essence, independent of all that surrounds them. This is also the attitude that unfortunately inspires the ambitions of many information scientists.

It is precisely this desire to establish impenetrable frontiers and unshakable foundations, Bachelard (1985: 41, 116) argues, that distinguishes the old from the new scientific spirit. The practices of contemporary science entail a 'diversification of axiomatics' and the recognition of an 'irreducible multiplicity of basic hypotheses'. The complexity of the manifold reality of contemporary science renders the idea of autonomy inoperative. What has changed is the relation of identity to non-identity, of inclusion to exclusion. The concepts and constructs of the new scientific spirit are relational rather than substantial and, as such, irreducibly heterogeneous. Bachelard's famous notion of an 'epistemological break' is hereby demonstrated.

Along similar lines, Bohm and Peat (1989: 26−7) have made some remarkable observations regarding this 'new spirit'. They ask a very important question: 'How can this new order ever get started?' Their answer is as follows:

> Both individually and socially, consciousness is rigidly conditioned by a host of assumptions that lead to their own concealment through false play. In the resulting confusion and illusion, the mind is not even able to be aware of these assumptions, or to give proper attention to them. Various ways have already been suggested in which the mind may be able to 'loosen' some of these assumptions. The essential point, however, is that any kind of free movement of the mind creates the opportunity for revealing and loosening the rigid assumptions that block creativity.

A further formidable contribution came from Prigogine and Stengers (1986) with their idea of 'a new alliance'. These authors are, respectively, a chemist who has won the Nobel Prize for Chemistry, and a philosopher of science of some considerable standing in Europe. The 'new alliance' they wish to promote is one between the human sciences and the natural sciences, on the basis that there are more things linking the two than separating them. These links should be articulated constructively.

Prigogine and Stengers's (1989) subsequent book addresses the problem of time and eternity and discusses the 'new place of the human being in the natural sciences'. Their dealing with determinism and indeterminism brings us very close to the focus of this chapter and this book. They emphasise that the world of classical science, in terms of which the world is fully understandable, precisely reflects the nightmare announced by authors such as Kundera, Huxley and Orwell, according to whom this same world is an irreducibly multiple world (Prigogine and Stengers, 1989: 80−1). These two notions and the way they are understood are self-evidently relevant to our field from the perspective of knowledge and information, but even more so from the perspective of ICTs and the way they are sometimes related to 'technological determinism'.

The notion of the 'instructed third' was developed by Michel Serres (1989, 1997). This idea is constantly intriguing in terms of its vitality, exuberance and inventive possibilities. It is also an additional significant effort to work out and establish the inevitable, but also fruitful, connections between knowledges. Serres' emphasis is on the linkages which are so difficult to identify but necessary and of vital importance to be pursued and promoted between the sciences, the humanities and philosophy, especially in view of the ways in which they complement and enrich each other. His famous viewpoint is that there is more fiction in science and more science in fiction than we are inclined to admit. This approach, perhaps more than any of the others, opens the way to inventiveness – the issue that enables people to move forward as individuals, but also as groups, societies and communities, by inventing new worlds, new meanings and new futures. It is also in full compliance with the alternative articulation of human thinking emphasised earlier. This brings me close to the dream I have for both information science and information work.

Two possible approaches to science emerge if we carefully follow the argument of Stengers (2000). From the above discussions it is clear that a new scientific spirit is embraced and actively promoted by some, with the implication of a choice between two approaches: deterministic versus indeterministic, stagnant versus creative, royal versus ambulant or nomad (Stengers, 2000: 154–5). With reference to Deleuze and Guattari she distinguishes between a royal science and an ambulant science:

> *Royal science is inseparable from a 'hylomorphic' model, implying both a form that organizes matter and a matter prepared for a form. Royal science does not make the 'ambulant' or 'nomad' sciences that preceded it disappear. The nomad sciences do not link science and power. Nor do they destine science to an autonomous development, because they were in solidarity with their terrain of exploration, because their practices were distributed according to the problems provoked by a singularized material, without having the power to assess the difference between what, from singularities, refers to 'matter itself' and what refers to the convictions and ambitions of the practitioners ... Royal science mobilizes the ambulant process. In the field of interaction of the two sciences, the ambulant sciences confine themselves to* inventing problems *whose solution is tied to a whole set of collective, non-scientific practices but whose* scientific solution *depends, on the contrary, on royal science and the way it has transformed the problem by introducing it into its theorematic apparatus and its organization of work.*
>
> *(Stengers, 2000: 154–5).*

What we find here is a 'demobilisation' of the positive sciences and this has to be linked to the question of complexity. These insights should be taken seriously by all scientists, and by information scientists in particular.

## 2.5  Challenges to information science

Information science faces comprehensive challenges. Our first and very natural question is: what are the implications of such a new or different approach to science for information science? Can information science remain satisfied with a traditional or classical scientific approach, or does it need some drastic and thorough rethinking? If this is undoubtedly required of the sciences due to the landscape changes, it is in a similar way but much more intensely required of information science in view of its specific focus and activity. The option is open: stay as we are, keeping as closely as possible to the classical tradition and run the risk of stagnation, or renew and rethink in order to become the culmination point of inventiveness!

My suggestion is that these changes pose, in turn, such serious and comprehensive challenges with such enormous opportunities that we owe it to our subject field to respond with as much intellectual input as we can. This consequently requires a radical rethinking of the place, focus, role and responsibility of the information sciences if we are to give an adequate account of the exciting prospects facing our science, and if we want to actively participate in the project of 'inventing the future' (Hannah & Harris, 1999).

What does this imply? It implies that the previously described developments and emphases should be taken seriously and explored further in the context of information science.

The first step would be the rethinking of information science along the lines suggested for the sciences in general by authors such as Bachelard, Bohm and Peat, Castoriades, Morin, and Prigogine and Stengers, to name but a few. The next two chapters will bring forward more names, whose work relates more directly to information science. Information scientists should give an account for themselves about these dramatic events in the field of science that force us to explore to the full the new scientific spirit, indeterminism, creativity and the approach proposed by nomadism. We as information scientists should ourselves give account of these dramatic events in the field of science that force us to fully explore the implications of the new scientific spirit while taking heed of the importance of the ongoing commuting between the royal and the ambulant aspects of our science. These views are on the table for us all to review as a matter of urgent necessity; they are complementary to the rethinking of human subjectivity and to the rethinking of thinking itself.

It would make sense to link the response to this challenge to the notion of 'paradigm' as developed by Morin (1983). What this means is that we should take the activity of reflection by the active mind seriously, with the full input of our intellectual capacity, without losing sight of the fact that this active mind is inserted into a dynamic network with powerful implications for its activity. We have to grasp and articulate the human depth of the paradigm, covering the idea of the Gordian knot and of the noological dynamics as the scene of the link between the sciences, human and natural, while, at the same time, keeping in mind the fact that the notion of a paradigm represents much more than simply a switch in methodical approach, philosophical direction or personal preference. As Morin himself puts it:

> *We have sought a grounding for human science in the science of nature ... But that led us to the conclusion that the science of nature must be based on a science of knowledge which is that of the knowing mind. That science, therefore, takes us back to the science of man, because the human mind, the human subject, must be understood as anthropo-social-cultural realities; i.e. the science of nature calls for a fundamental anthropology ... In this encounter, the science of mind gives rise to a noology which itself bursts open in a complex way: on the one hand, a branch that calls for a noological science and in which noo-organization refers us back to*

*the theory of auto-eco-organization; on the other hand, a branch which is logical, ideological, semiotic, linguistic … We are thus back to the real complexity of an unheard-of interpenetration, via the sciences of mind or noology, between natural sciences and human sciences; at the same time we are led to a kind of arrangement, a mutual dependency and a dual, reciprocally satellite rotation between natural sciences and human sciences, one the servant-mistress of the other, one the epistemologization of the other, but on the understanding that they be hoisted to the meta-level of complex epistemology. From then on, we will have to conceive of epistemology as a circuit, but we will also be required to consider that there is likewise a Gordian knot, where everything is tied together … The direction of our thinking can be considered as a sort of parade review of the multi-determined character of knowledge. The latter always has determinations which are individual, bio-anthropological, noological, i.e. linguistic, logical and ideological; sociocultural; and one could and should add other determinations which overlap the above, such as psychoanalytical, material … These determinations … coagulate and agglomerate in any field of knowledge and thought inquiry … [and] are also, in a certain way, fundamentally related in deep structure, and … the Gordian knot of these multiple interrelations between various insistencies which govern knowledge, also conceal an underlying nucleus where … strong forces are at work. Here the notion of paradigm steps in at the very heart of the idea of knowledge and of scientific theory. Science is not purely and simply the accumulation of factual knowledge, but is structured by theories which, in order to structure the knowledge, bring to bear inherently ideological structurations. (1983: 11−12)*

The next step would be to look at the contributions of information scientists themselves. Contemporary scientific approaches to information science, such as the rational, the socio-behavioural, the cognitive, the sense-making and the hermeneutic, as summarised by Ingwersen (1992: 306−9), may be a starting point because they offer us a significant opening. The 'argumentation for abandoning the rationalistic tradition and the reasons for moving into a human-based hermeneutical attitude to information design and processing problems' has been reiterated. Ingwersen further emphasises that every phenomenon, domain or dimension studied in information science can be approached from one of these scientific views or approaches while, at the same time, illustrating their complementary nature. An obvious consequence, as highlighted by Ingwersen, would be that a methodological pluralism be adopted for most investigations in our field.

This view is reinforced by Bougnoux (1993) with reference to a number of disciplines relevant to the information and communication sciences. His work on the 'birth of an interdiscipline' is arranged around the following eight fields: philosophical approaches; the empire of signs or semiotics; speech act theories; the dreams of the masses; the mechanisation of the mind; mediological openings; the logic of transmissions; and the embodiment of communities. The implications of the interconnectedness between these fields and information science and work need to be worked out and explored in full. These emphases, with the implied nomadic movement between the diverse disciplines, nevertheless make of information science, as an interscience or interdiscipline, one of the most exciting, rich and highly relevant intellectual and scientific exploratory endeavours thinkable in our contemporary and very challenging times.

Wersig's (1990) views about a number of things need to be explored because of their relevance for reflection in our context. His articulation of the difference between 'calculus' and 'aesthesis', in which it is emphasised how the human being is much more than a mere calculating being, but also one with the potential of aesthetics that go far beyond rational calculations, adds a worthwhile dimension to the place of humans in our scientific and professional context which is too easily neglected. Wersig's (1990: 184−7) suggestion is that the situation should be reversed from the suppressing rationalisation of the sciences with a focus on information for calculi, to a liberating opening up to the provision of 'more knowledge for humans' which finds expression in his proposal of 'a back to knowledge' direction.

In another article, in which Wersig (1992) sketches 'a weaver bird's perspective' of information science, he emphasises that the main focus of information science should be the interweaving of the scientific approaches highlighted by Ingwersen, the broad intellectual fields demarcated by Bougnoux and the interconcepts that are present and relevant to all intellectual work in all domains or disciplines. This extensive establishment of connections and links between knowledges paves the way for the idea of a postmodem science (Wersig, 1993b) to the displeasure of many. Or, in the context of this study, it may be interpreted as an effort towards the birth of an interscience or an interdiscipline. The idea of the role of interconcepts (Wersig, 1992, 1993a) provides the means by which the interscientific activity can really proceed and make progress.

Related to and valuable for the views above, although not that of an information scientist, is the work done by Pierre Lévy. His contributions to collective intelligence (1997), virtual reality (1998), a world philosophy (2000) and cyberculture (2001) have a remarkable relevance to the intellectual and knowledge work to be done by information scientists and information professionals in the context of a newly shaped interscience focus. The wealth of his contributions offers hope for the future of humankind, despite the many arguments that claim a hopeless future.

## 2.6    Information science: its functioning and responsibility

The explication of the relevance of these insights for information science, with a view to its functioning and its responsibility, is now required.

### 2.6.1    Its functioning

All sciences are engaged in thinking − so is information science. A difference in thinking, as well as in our understanding of human thinking, is required − not different in terms of the thought potential of humans, but different in terms of the restrictive and reductionistic conceptions of thinking. This reductionistic conception of human thinking is particularly influential in the field of science and needs to be eradicated. Information science unfortunately fits too easily into and complies much too easily with this reductionistic approach and these restrictive strategies, probably as a result of a lack of sufficiently clear and thorough reflection on its position.

We need to explore a number of examples that stress, from different perspectives, clear 'irreductionistic' approaches (a term borrowed from Latour, 1988) to thinking (also see Chapter 4). The revision of what is understood by human subjectivity goes together with these views and adds some special dynamics to the whole issue of thinking. The views of Baudrillard (1989), Wersig (1990, 1993a), Lévy (1993), Hayles (1999) and Fukuyama (2002) offer excellent guidelines in this regard. Unless we can develop an adequate understanding of the human being (as thinker, scientist and knowledge worker), we will, in view of recent developments and landscape changes, probably not be able to comply with the worldwide demands of this century.

In terms of the tradition of defining the sciences according to object and method, information science may appear to encounter difficulties in being defined as a science. At the same time, because of its positioning between or 'in the *inter* of the media and the disciplines', it qualifies as a unique kind of scientific and intellectual endeavour that can be called an interscience. As an interscience, it should adopt, as its final ambition, the overcoming of the divorce and distrust between disciplines and sciences. Its position reminds one of the position taken up by, and also given to, philosophy. It should be working within and between the sciences, applying and utilising 'interconcepts' with the full capacity of human thinking in an irreductionistic way, thus weaving insights and knowledges together into significant networks.

The real issue at stake is the consideration of information science not only as an interscience, but also as a nomad science in the true sense of the word. Deleuze and Guattari (1987) offer an exemplary characterisation of a nomad science. (See Stengers (2000) for a discussion of their views as discussed earlier.) Lévy is equally explicit and borrows from these authors when he writes:

> We have again become nomads. By this I am not referring to pleasure cruises, exotic vacations, or tourism. Nor to the incessant come and go of businessmen and harried travellers ... Movement no longer means travelling from point to point on the surface of the globe, but crossing universes of problems, lived worlds, landscapes of meaning ... The nomadism of today reflects the continuous and rapid transformation of scientific, technical, economic, professional and mental landscapes. Even if we remain rooted to one spot the world will change around us. Yet we move. And the chaotic mass of our responses produces a general transformation. (1997: xxii–xxiii)

If René Thom, the well-known French mathematician, can speak of a 'nomadic mathematics' (Stengers, 2000: 156), how much easier it would be to speak of a 'nomadic informatology'. The vocation is not to reduce the multiplicity of sensible phenomena to the unity of mathematical or informatological description, but to construct an intelligibility of qualitative differences within which to move.

The establishment of connections and links with a variety of 'disciplines' such as semiology, mediology, psychoanalysis, philosophy, speech act theory, artificial intelligence, pragmatics, cybernetics and so forth (as explored by Bougnoux, 1993) is at issue here because of the importance of all these matters for the consideration of information and the possibilities of its application. Information science, given its unique position in the gallery of sciences and intellectual exercises, could play a decisive role in the establishment of these necessary connections. The fragmentation of knowledge and the animosity between knowledges and their suspicions of each other are, to a great extent, responsible for the many failures in knowledge work and knowledge applications. Commitment in the information sciences to overcoming these barriers and facilitating connections and links can contribute to overcoming many of the obstacles blocking the road to knowledge use.

## 2.6.2   Its responsibility

In more than one respect the information scientist, together with the information professional, has a number of challenging and unique responsibilities.

The first is to firmly reject dishonesty in science, by which is meant the reductionistic dispositions that we inculcate and shamelessly promote among our students and among information workers. This approach misleads everybody – students, researchers and teachers. (See LaFollette (1998) on 'scientific misconduct' in this regard, although her article has a somewhat different focus.)

Meaningful information (what counts) needs to be elaborated on, and not merely be seen as information as such. Strategies for finding and promoting meaningful information are among our most important responsibilities, given the immense information overload facing us.

A culture of knowledge needs to be cultivated. Who will and can do this if we refuse to do it? Wersig (1990) and Bonaventura (1997) write convincingly about this responsibility.

Comprehensive literacy needs to be promoted as this is the only guarantee for adequate reading and for the engagement in comprehensive, interscientific, nomadic thinking, which is desperately needed if we take what is entrusted to us seriously. In this regard, see De Beer (2014), who writes about different modes of reading, and Burnett (2002), who writes about rhizomorphic reading as ergodic literacy. When Serres (1997), the acritical reader, states that 'reading is a journey', he certainly expresses the true spirit of the interscientific, nomadic activity.

The focus of the information sciences and information work and services should, in the last analysis, be informatisation. As Wersig (1993a) puts it, informatisation becomes known as the process in which the mega-trends are indicated by the three key terms 'application explosion', 'integration' and 'mass distribution'. As this process increases, the information derived from knowledge structures can be represented by multiple media.

The most unique feature of establishing links and building connections within the framework of knowledge networks, as spelled out earlier, is the potential this offers for inventiveness on a grand scale. It should never be forgotten that inventiveness is an intellectual endeavour par excellence. In the final analysis, it depends on the imagination of teachers and researchers in the field to give this interscience the place it deserves.

The next two chapters take the views touched on in this chapter in a more substantial way a little further and show how the crises of the sciences demand a rethinking of the sciences and how this rethinking of the sciences has specific challenges and promises for the possibility of the rethinking of information science as well.

# References

Bachelard, G. (1985). *The new scientific spirit*. New York: Beacon Press.

Baudrillard, J. (1989). Videowelt und fraktales Subjekt. In Ars Electronica (Ed.), *Philosophien der neue Technologie*. Berlin: Merve Verlag.

Belkin, N. (1978). Information concepts for information science. *Journal of Documentation*, *34*, 55–85.

Bohm, D., & Peat, F. D. (1989). *Science, order and creativity*. London: Routledge.

Bonaventura, M. (1997). The benefits of a knowledge culture. *Aslib Proceedings*, *49*(4), 82–89.

Bougnoux, D. (1993). *Sciences de l'information et de la communication*. Paris: Larousse.

Burnett, K. (2002). Rhizomorphic reading: An ergodic literacy. In A. Kent, & C. M. Hall (Eds.), *Encyclopaedia of library and information science* (Vol. 72, Suppl. 35). New York: Marcel Dekker.

Callon, M. (1989). *La science et ses réseaux: Genèse et circulation de faits scientifiques*. Paris: La Découverte.

Castoriades, C. (1984). *Crossroads in the Labyrinth*. Brighton: Harvester Press.

De Beer, C. S. (1996). Let the new knowledge come. *South African Journal for Higher Education*, *10*(2), 75–85.

De Beer, C. S. (2001). Atlas of knowledges: In pursuit of new knowledge. *Mousaion*, *19*(1), 35–52.

De Beer, C. S. (2003). The new knowledge dispensation. *Mousaion*, *21*(2), 106–127.

De Beer, C. S. (2014). Reading: The understanding and invention of meaning. In J. S. Wessels, & J. C. Pauw (Eds.), *Reflective public administration: Context, knowledge and methods*. Pretoria: Unisa Press.

Deleuze, G., & Guattari, F. (1987). *A thousand plateaus: Capitalism and schizophrenia*. London: Athlone Press.

Fukuyama, F. (2002). *Our posthuman future: Consequences of the biotechnology revolution*. New York: Farrar, Straus & Giroux.

Hannah, S. A., & Harris, M. H. (1999). *Inventing the future: Information services for a new millennium*. Stanford, CT: Ablex.

Hayles, N. K. (1999). *How we became posthuman: Virtual bodies in cybernetics, literature, and informatics*. Chicago: University of Chicago Press.

Ingwersen, P. (1992). Conceptions of information science. In P. Vakkari, & B. Cronin (Eds.), *Conceptions of library and information science: Historical, empirical and theoretical perspectives*. London: Taylor Graham.

Ingwersen, P. (1995). Information and information science. In A. Kent, & C. M. Hall (Eds.), *Encyclopaedia of library and information science* (Vol. 56, Suppl. 19). New York: Marcel Dekker.

Kochen, M. (1983). Library science and information science – broad or narrow? In F. Machlup, & U. Mansfield (Eds.), *The study of information: Interdisciplinary messages*. New York: Wiley.

Kuhlen, R. (1990). Zum Stand pragmatischer Forschung in der Informationswissenschaft. In J. Herget, & R. Kuhlen (Eds.), *Pragmatische aspekte beim entwurf und betreib von informationssystemen*. Konstanz: Universitätsverlag.

LaFollette, M. (1998). Scientific misconduct. In A. Kent, & C. M. Hall (Eds.), *Encyclopaedia of library and information science* (Vol. 68, Suppl. 31). New York: Marcel Dekker.

Latour, B. (1987). *Science in action*. London: Open University Press.

Latour, B. (1988). *The pasteurization of France*. Cambridge, MA: Harvard University Press.

Lévy, P. (1993). Les technologies de l'intelligence: l'avenir de la pensée à l'ère informatique. Paris: La Decouverte.

Lévy, P. (1997). *Collective intelligence: Mankind's emerging world in cyberspace*. New York: Plenum Trade.

Lévy, P. (1998). *Becoming virtual: Reality in the digital age*. New York: Plenum Trade.

Lévy, P. (2000). *World philosophie: Le marché, le cyberespace, la conscience*. Paris: Editions Odile Jacob.

Lévy, P. (2001). *Cyberculture*. Minneapolis, MN: University of Minnesota Press.

Morin, E. (1983). Social paradigms of scientific knowledge. *SubStance, 39*, 3–20.

Parrochia, D. (Ed.), (2001). *Penser les réseaux*. Seyssel: Editions Champ Vallon.

Prigogine, I., & Stengers, I. (1986). *Order out of chaos*. New York: Beacon Press.

Prigogine, I., & Stengers, I. (1989). *Tussen tijd en eeuwigheid: De nieuwe plaats van de mens in de natuurwetenschap*. Amsterdam: Bert Bakker.

Saracevic, T. (1999). Information science. *Journal of the American Society for Information Science, 50*(12), 1051–1063.

Serres, M. (1989). Literature and the exact sciences. *SubStance, 18*(2), 3–34.

Serres, M. (1994). *Atlas*. Paris: Julliard.

Serres, M. (1997). *The troubadour of knowledge*. Ann Arbor, MI: University of Michigan Press.

Steiner, G. (1999). *Barbarie de l'ignorance*. La Tour d'Aigues: Éditions de l'Aube.

Stengers, I. (2000). *The invention of modern science*. Minneapolis, MN: University of Minnesota Press.

Stiegler, B. (2010). *Taking care of youth and the generations*. Stanford, CA: Stanford University Press.

Vakkari, P. (1994). Library and information science: Its content and scope. In L. P. Godden (Ed.), *Advances in librarianship* (Vol. 18). New York: Academic Press.

Vakkari, P., & Cronin, B. (Eds.), (1992). *Conceptions of library and information science: Historical, empirical and theoretical perspectives*. London: Taylor Graham.

Wersig, G. (1990). The changing role of knowledge in an information society. In D. J. Fosl (Ed.), *The information environment: A world view*. New York: Elsevier Scientific.

Wersig, G. (1992). Information science and theory: A weaver bird's perspective. In P. Vakkari, & B. Cronin (Eds.), *Conceptions of library and information science*. London: Taylor Graham.

Wersig, G. (1993a). *Fokus mensch: Bezugspunkte postmoderner wissenschift: Wissen, kommunikation, kultur*. Frankfurt am Main: Peter Lang.

Wersig, G. (1993b). Information science: The study of postmodern knowledge. *Information processing and management, 29*(2), 229–239.

# Information science in a post-scientific position

**3**

## Part 1: The limitations of science and information science

## 3.1 Introduction

In 1936 the philosopher, Edmund Husserl (1970), wrote a very thoughtful article on what he called 'The Crisis of the European Sciences'. This became a famous and much quoted article. The core of the crisis that he describes can be articulated in the following way. Is the crisis of the sciences not an exaggeration? After all, 'crisis' suggests that the scientific character, the way it sets its task, the development of a methodology, is questionable. The whole direction of the enquiry, the general evaluation, must be changed. 'It concerns not the scientific character of the sciences but rather what they, or what science in general, had meant and could mean for human existence' (Husserl, 1970: 5). It may indeed have something to do with the 'scientific character' in the sense that the positive reduction of the idea of science to mere 'factual science, creates, or forces upon us, blind spots, unclarities, regarding issues that are required for life.' The crisis of science in this regard may imply then 'the loss of its meaning for life, for human existence' (Husserl, 1970: 5). In the process the crisis of science could increasingly lead to the crisis of European humanity itself concerning the total meaningfulness of its cultural life, its total existence. The focus on 'factual science' creates 'a loss of the one all-encompassing science, the science of the totality of that which is', the loss of knowing for the sake of knowledge entities and eventually information entities. 'Merely fact-minded sciences make merely fact-minded people' (Husserl, 1970: 6). This means that 'in our vital need this science has nothing to say to us. It excludes in principle precisely the questions which man [the human being], given over in our unhappy times to the most portentous upheavals, finds the most burning: questions of the meaning or meaninglessness of the whole of this human existence' (Husserl, 1970: 6).

These questions are universal and imperative for all human beings. They demand universal reflections and answers based on rational [and noological] insight (see De Beer, 2011). These questions concern human beings as free and self-determining beings in their actions on and behaviour towards the surrounding human and extra-human world, a freedom that enables humans to rationally and noologically shape themselves and their surrounding worlds. World-creation and world-enchantment are the most special capacity humans possess. What does factual science in its dogmatic fixity have to say about human freedom and about reason and unreason, about noology and the noosphere?

The mere sciences of facts and of bodies have nothing to say. 'Scientific, objective truth is exclusively a matter of establishing what the world, the physical as well as the spiritual world, is in fact' (Husserl, 1970: 6). But if the sciences only acknowledge what is objectively established in this fashion, and if history has nothing more to teach us than that all the shapes of the spiritual world, all the conditions of life, the ideals, the norms upon which human beings rely, form and dissolve themselves like fleeting waves, that it always was and ever will be so, can the world and human beings in it truthfully have a meaning, and is it not unavoidable that again and again that reason must turn into nonsense, and well-being into misery? Can we live in this world, Husserl asks, where historical events are nothing but an unending concatenation of illusory progress and bitter disappointment? The rigorous scientific character requires that the scholar carefully excludes all valuative positions, all questions of reason and unreason, of noology and pathology related to human subject matter and its cultural configurations in terms of which meaning is to be established (see Husserl, 1970: 6–7).

The crucial question is whether this is not the same problem as what can be called 'the crisis in information science'? Cronin (1995: 45) calls it a 'deeper professional malaise'. Due to the fact that information science tries to comply with the standardised version of the sciences as mere factual sciences, it misses, like other sciences, the same essential issues related to a humane world, human meaning and the comprehensive needs of a 'total human existence'. This is rather sad. The fortunate thing is that if this is the case it can certainly be rectified. The process of rectification, however, requires and demands serious commitment since we are called upon to apply our full rational and noological, that is spiritual, capacities. Are we ready for this? The general rethinking requires a drastic rethinking of science and scientific approaches, and of course a rethinking of information science. This endeavour is challenging and will make those who accept this challenge unpopular. Again: are we ready and prepared for this? Section 3.4 and Chapter 4 respectively attend to this process of rethinking science in general and information science in particular. What is really needed is very explicit conceptual equipment that will enable us to work into new, totally different and more fruitful and inventive directions (Chapter 4). Numerous examples can be followed in this regard (see Roux & De Beer, 2010a, 2010b, 2011, and especially the reference lists in these articles).

## 3.2 The traditional, generally accepted conception of science

The so-called traditional, that is the generally accepted or conventional notion of science, what Husserl called 'fact-minded science', is built on certain definite assumptions about reality as object and its knowability, the subject and its knowing capacity, knowledge and its depths and boundaries. These assumptions have only limited validity and are no longer absolutely valid as many would claim (if ever they had any absolute validity at any point in time), in terms of many recent (20 to 30 years) approaches, and should urgently be reconsidered. Before any rethinking of science can be pursued or any new name for an alternative conception of science can be considered or contemplated, as Bohm (in Bohm & Peat, 1989) justifiably suggested, it will be useful to consider the notion of science proper in the sense given to it in the context of scientific realism. Bacon in his *Novum Organum*, where the idea of 'knowledge is power' originates, emphasises the importance of the subject/object division and especially the emphasis on the mastery of objects by subjects in a rigidly methodical way. In this context the real is fixed, the method is straightforward and knowledge, generated in this way, is final. This went on for centuries. In this context reality is considered to be fairly static, programmed, predictable, determined, and which is even true of human reality. Bohm (in Bohm & Peat, 1989: 12−13) emphasises very strongly the fragmentary nature of disciplinary work as the unfortunate consequence of these views, but at the same time with its own implied negative consequences for solving problems and creating meaning, in the sense that worse problems have been created than before, and that life seems, for many, to have lost its meaning.

Midgley (1991) emphasises that science in general, in the conventional sense, due to specialisation, forces us into narrowness. Sciences in the professional contexts, where the requirements of the professions (especially their practices) compel them for the sake of compliance to become prescriptive, are forcing us into even more and deeper narrowness. Practitioners very often boast about their unwillingness and of necessity their inability to think − proud of the inability to think they turn the situation into a laughing matter. Narrowness is the manifestation and also the humus for narrow-mindedness which creates insecurity, a feeling of threat, and eventually culminates in obsessiveness, the blurring of vision and the loss of enthusiasm. This situation is dangerous, fatal and destructive, but also powerless, as may be expected, to deal with conflicts. In the process dangerous facts and pernicious theories are created or perhaps rather fabricated. (See Ballay (2010) and even Laszlo (1989) much earlier on this issue of the incapacity of problem solving despite all the pretensions to the contrary.) The fatal combination of one-sidedness, universal pretension and sensationalism (the characteristics of ideology), as emphasised by Midgley, are the necessary consequences of these developments.

Michel Henry (2012) is equally harsh on the limitations of the general scientific endeavour. He places it in the context of what he called 'the ideology of barbarism'. Henry (2012:75) writes:

> One should include all types of thoughts that are lived and experienced as knowledge of the 'real' and 'true' being when one is preoccupied exclusively with objective being, that is to say, with what can and must be brought before them through their procedures ... Such thoughts do not only posit themselves as sciences but as the only possible science.

This means: nothing else is science; moreover, nothing else is knowledge, but only this kind of knowledge. What is more: in this process we have reduced knowledge to something manageable which can be handled and measured, similar to our handling of objects and things, to our benefit and not as something that changes us and transforms us. '... [W]hat is given as an object is already of a reduced nature — in other words nature is no longer what it is meant to be — the Galilian nature of the people of our times. This is in fact what allows us to define both these peoples and these times' (Henry, 2012: 75). It is quite frightening to realise that our view of science forces us to define whatever else in those terms.

*The progress of the sciences of objects is guided by the acquired results through the use of methods. To the thematic emptiness, that is the truth of this development of objects as reductions, the same uncertainty and the same anarchy is added on the level of method ... Method ultimately merges with science. Just like a science, every method can be defined on the basis of the object that it seeks to elucidate. The object dictates the science.*

*(Henry, 2012: 77)*

Take note of Michel Serres' remark on method:

*Who is more profoundly boring than the repetitive reasoner who copies or seems to construct by constantly repositioning the same cube? Ruminating on the past — what a system! Repeating a method — what laziness! Method seeks but does not find. Henry considers these types of reductionistic thought to represent 'the ideology of barbarism'. (1997: 100)*

Objective reality, what Henry calls 'objective being', is reversible and deterministic. Lyotard (1995) is very specific about the limitations, even dangerous limitations, of this deterministic view of science, which cause a crisis. Lyotard will serve as the example of the suggested post-scientific position for information science. In a remarkably clear essay, 'The Contemporary Pragmatics of Scientific Knowledge', he states that 'scientific knowledge is seeking a "crisis resolution" — a resolution of the crisis of determinism' (Lyotard, 1995: 165). This immediately reminds us of Husserl and the crisis of the European sciences. Why is determinism a crisis? If we think of the input/output ratio, or of the cause/effect strategy, the assumption or presupposition is that the system into which input is entered, or onto which cause is forced, is a stable system. This system follows a regular, expected path where accurate predictions are possible. The outcome is determined and we should know what to expect. This is precisely the positivist approach against which certain information scientists vehemently protest (see, for example, Day, 2004, 2008; Frohmann, 1994; Wersig, 1993a, 1993b). It should be kept in mind, as suggested by Henry, that our view of science determines and defines all related entities, activities and the strategies of all subdisciplines as well as our policies and the directions we take, and, of course, all our practices. This is exactly why meaning, the full human existence, knowledge in its multiple fullness, and compositional thinking are outdefined from our disciplinary vocabulary which has landed us in a severe crisis. Bohm (2009: 127) refers to this objectivist, mechanistic and deterministic approach in science as 'destructive' and as having 'bad effects'. Others, such as Stengers (2009), would use even stronger language and refer to 'the catastrophic effects'.

Virilio (2000), in a much later publication, attacks the classic conception of science and indicates the extent to which it is from a certain perspective a fruitless endeavour and, in addition to that, shows how it opens the way for a distorted conception of information after which he introduces the very possibility of what he calls 'the information bomb', less visible but more destructive than the first bomb, namely the atomic bomb. Why more destructive? The atomic bomb is local and affects only a relatively small group of people and causes mainly bodily harm. The information bomb is not local but universal, it affects not only individuals but whole societies and eventually humanity itself, and it is a spiritual matter causing spiritual and mental damage. Dealing effectively with this threat poses a severe challenge to information scientists and workers. This cannot be done physically and empirically, but intellectually and consequently also spiritually. But for them to be able to engage in science in this way they should at least grasp the problems posed by the classical notion of science.

The classical conception of science opens the way. How? Virilio writes:

*If truth is what is verifiable, the truth of contemporary science is not so much the extent of progress achieved as the scale of technical catastrophes occasioned. Science, after having been carried along for almost half a century in the arms race of the East—West deterrence era, has developed solely with a view to the pursuit of* limit-performances, *to the detriment of any effort to discover a coherent truth useful to humanity. Modern science, having progressively become* techno-science — *the product of the fatal confusion between the* operational instrument *and* exploratory research — *has ... lost its way ... (2000: 1)*

The inability 'to discover a coherent truth useful to humanity' strongly reminds us of Husserl's crisis. The information bomb as a consequence of this amplifies the process.

*Science which is not so attached to truth as it once was but more to immediate effectiveness, is now drifting towards its decline ... a fact concealed by the success of its devices and tools ... is losing itself in the very excessiveness of its alleged progress ... [T]echno-science is gradually wrecking the scholarly resources of all knowledge.*

*(Virillio, 2000: 2)*

The quotation from Rabelais 'Science without conscience is a mere ruination of the soul' (Virillio, 2000: 3) reminds us of the wonderful book by Edgar Morin, *Science with Conscience* (1990) in which he emphasises the exact opposite.

However, the fact remains that the dynamics of reality, life and more specifically human life are too complex to be understood and interpreted as being determined, or to be reduced to less than what it is. The idea of uncertainty is more prominent than certainty, enabling the physicist, Prigogine to write a book entitled *The End of Certainty* (1997) in which he writes extensively about determinism and indeterminism in order to emphasise the importance of indeterminism. Edgar Morin and others developed theories of complexity, chaos and the immeasurable related to the problem of uncertainty as part of the real. Even physical reality is to be understood as going far beyond reality as certain, fixed and predictable. Hereby emphasis is put on the possibility, but also the importance and necessity, of the rethinking of the scientific endeavour (see Bohm, in Bohm & Peat, 1989: 1—14). Rethinking science, and especially the subject-object relationship and the place and role of method as these entities feature in the modern scientific endeavour, may especially be of central importance in rethinking the scientific position of information science.

The fruitfulness of what we are engaged in is not determined by the amount of enthusiasm and activities we pursue, the amount of money we are sponsored with and the number of people that we engage, but by the depth and quality of our reflections and thought processes, as well as the issues that are addressed and how they are addressed and to what extent problems are really solved. We cannot proceed and succeed in terms of the flamboyancy of our PR strategies and practical and applied endeavours, but rather by the quality of the content and the theoretical soundness of our knowledge and scientific pursuits.

## 3.3   Information science seems to be out of step (and will remain out of step, unless ...)

Although information science tries hard to comply with the norms, requirements and prescriptions of 'the standardised view of science or research', its efforts have never been fully successful and this remains a matter of serious and continuous concern. In Europe, the Americas and Africa incisive questions are continuously being asked about the truly scientific nature of information science. What does it mean and what kind of science can it be? It simply cannot comply with the 'norms' and 'prescriptions' of the so-called fact-minded sciences. For these very reasons there are constantly recurring efforts at conferences and in journal articles to rethink the scientific nature of information science. The problem arises when efforts are made to define the object and method and even the subject. When this cannot be done in relatively clear terms as in physics or chemistry, for example, serious doubts and suspicions emerge related to its scientific nature and characteristics. In view of this information science seems to be out of step with the focus, strategies and protocol of scientific work in the traditional sense. It is not fit for that kind of approach. Most of the rethinking and redefinition we find are still efforts to bring it in line with this tradition, but in a fairly fruitless way, instead of contemplating alternative approaches. It constantly lands in dead-end streets, and remains far removed, like the sciences in general, from the meaningfulness of total human existence. Buckland (2011) is a recent example — in an effort to rethink but still trying to justify the generally accepted version of science he misses the point with his reference to the weakness or poverty of the 'inter' or the 'between' in view of the strength of the disciplines. In view of these critical issues information science flounders. It blocks instead of enhances meaning; it stifles thought instead of enthusiastically promoting it. But is this the only route, trying to save what cannot be saved? Small and regular efforts in re-articulation show the frustration with this keenness to comply and acknowledge that everything is not well with our 'discipline'.

A number of information scientists have identified and articulated this problem in detail: Cronin (1995) and Warner (2001) ask critical questions regarding this huge problem and make a number of useful suggestions to be taken seriously for the way forward, although it is clear that not many are keen to take them and their suggestions seriously. Wersig (1993a, 1993b), Frohmann (1994) and Day (2004, 2008) are equally, if not more, explicit. We have to read and study them and seriously consider their proposed strategies and approaches, and contemplate what they consider to be the shortcomings. If we are unwilling to do so and perpetuate what we have accepted we have to bear the consequences. The issue is not how busy we are as information scientists and information workers, but what kind of business we are engaged in.

What Midgley calls 'narrowness of science' and Henry describes as 'the barbarous implications of science' (a certain kind of science, in other words), Cronin (1995: 45) would call, in the context of information science, trying to comply with the traditional notion of science, 'intellectual blinkeredness and intolerance'. Wersig (1990) is concerned about the 'rubbish'-explosion with its concomitant growth of illiteracy and knowledge gaps as well as the depersonalisation, fragmentation and rationalisation of knowledge, all with their destructive implications for individuals and societies. Frohmann (1994: 11) feels that 'the identities that information science studies are seen as 'found' identities – given, natural, objective – and as such it fatally compromises avenues of criticism and the development of alternatives'; it blocks any possibility of new thinking about information science. Because information is viewed as an entity unto itself, rather than immersed in networks of relations giving meaning and value to it, Day (2004: 584–5) feels it can frankly be stated that the field of information science is a field that has suffered from a 'widespread amnesia of its own history' and that this forgetting may be part of the unfortunate epistemology of the modern conception of information.

The implications of these diagnoses are serious. Cronin characterises the consequences as follows, especially in view of his keenness to identify the core of our field by stating in the negative that

> *instead of a rich core of intellectually validated content wrapped in a light coating of professional norms and values [by which he clearly demonstrates the necessity of theory and intellectual work for practice in the profession], we have created a perversion in which the wrapping has become content; where an inchoate mass of pseudo-theory on ethics, socialization, professionalism, and feminism has moved to the core. Membrane has become central. (1995: 52)*

Bougnoux (1995: 75) emphasises that rigid or crystallised thinking in the context of information science and work does not contribute to information just as amorphous thought cannot make any contribution either. 'Information dies by the excess of closedness as well as by the excess of openness and lives by the compromise between these two extreme pitfalls of crystal and smoke' (See Henri Atlan (1986), the source of Bougnoux's view, in this regard.) An intermediary space is called for in view of any informational or semiotic relationship while a stimulus-response or cause-effect relationship (Lyotard's determinism in science mentioned previously) puts us on the edge of the grave.

And then Bougnoux continues:

> *Our first knowledges are glued to us, crystallised and henceforth solidary and solid,*
> *oppose itself effectively against concurrent or new informations. Our informational*
> *closure or closedness depends on our organic constitution, but also on our previous*
> *informations sedimented in doctrines, in systems, theories or ideologies. We are*
> *effectively locked up, imprisoned and the keys are thrown away. Unless we protect*
> *the openness and suppleness, and the free movement within the vast space between*
> *the extremes, we may find that our dearest knowledges may create obstacles to*
> *others, especially new ones. How do we learn what really counts? In other words,*
> *that which really promotes meaning, the meaning that is so often absent or missing?*
> *We become sterile and without influence. We become powerless to the challenge to*
> *release the power of words and to activate symbolic acuteness and formative power.*
> *It is necessary to underline how much information is by nature scattered, evasive,*
> *irregular or misplaced. (1995: 73, my translation)*

Information, says Bougnoux, is a strange notion and so easily perverted (1995: 73)! Many people play games with it and use and abuse it to their heart's content, which easily contributes to the perversion.

The frightening conclusion is that key subdisciplines, such as user studies, user needs, information-seeking behaviour, information behaviour, information retrieval, readership, even record studies, knowledge management and information ethics, are defined in these terms, as far as both their theoretical and their practical sides are concerned. Both Frohmann (1995) and Day (2004) strongly emphasise the very important point, namely that depending on our view of science we will define all the relevant scientific subdisciplines accordingly, which means that the narrowness, rigidity, barbaric ideology, malaise and so forth that define our science will automatically also define all the subdisciplines. Julian Warner (2001: 251) emphasises 'theoretical impoverishment', 'lack of conceptual awareness', unwillingness to commit to the 'familiarisation with major contributions' (of an intellectual nature) flawed by intellectual laziness', as some of the major consequences of the keenness to associate with the positivistic, empiristic, scientist notion of the sciences in general, to use the formulations of Day (2004).

Hereby the problems related to 'the crisis of meaning' pertaining to the sciences in general are in a similar way transferred to information science and all its sub-disciplines, and as such they become equal producers of these problems. The implication: 'The basic difficulty is that our practice is unaware of the fact that it is producing all these problems' (Bohm, 2009: 142). We have to transform our sciences into new sciences before this can change. The renewal cannot and 'does not begin with a practice. *Practice must follow out of something deeper*' (Bohm, 2009: 143). This 'something deeper' is neglected in favour of 'an overemphasis on productivity ... and an overemphasis on quantitative analyses' (Day, 2004: 592−3), and a single focus on economic values, of course.

Such statements enhance the challenges posed to information/knowledge workers to invent something sensible and meaningful. From these arguments it is clear that it would be wise for information science to rethink in a radical way its scientific nature and status with a view to a significant future. The possibility of information science to engage in the process of rethinking its own position may find some substantial inspiration from the processes of new thinking in the sciences.

What are the ways to defeat this threatening challenge? We have to rethink, and thoroughly rethink, science and especially information science and the implications of this rethinking for information and knowledge work. We have to force our way back towards comprehensive usefulness, towards meaning, while realising that the total existence of humans is at stake. Unless we do so the crisis of information science will certainly deepen. Information science will remain out of step with the sciences as generally accepted; it will remain uncertain about its identity as a science; and it will struggle to identify with the sciences rethought. The rethinking of the sciences in general should guide us on our way forward.

## 3.4 Thinking differently about science

The fundamental criticism raised by both outsiders and scientists themselves relates to the limitations of the standardised and generally accepted scientific approach that more or less all of us are forced to embrace, as empiricist and positivist, and consequently reductionistic, one-sided and short-sighted. What remain are no longer scientific but research projects along the lines sketched in Section 3.2, pretending to qualify as being fully scientific. This approach leaves aside so much of the most decisive factors and aspects of reality and all the practical activities are completely disabled when they do not accommodate these aspects. At the same time, as part of the process, this strategy eliminates both human and humane foci. This is the main reason for Husserl's crisis of the sciences. Fortunately, alternative approaches exist and are promoted by many with the exact view to accommodate these neglected elements which are avoided, and in doing so strive to eliminate the shortcomings or limitations and the 'bad effects' caused by this neglect. All the sciences, despite the firm convictions surrounding and supporting them, are no longer purely successful and guaranteed. Many outcomes are questionable and even dangerous. In view of this the sciences are questioned and criticised. The same is true of information science. It should be realised that there is not just one, properly and finally standardised, way of thinking about science. In other words there is not just one valid conception of science, whether for philosophers reflecting on science and its nature, or for the many scientists of an international standing reflecting on their activities. On the strength of these alternative views and approaches that will briefly be attended to I want eventually to link up and suggest an alternative scientific approach in Chapter 4 for information science as well.

The urge to think differently about the sciences is certainly gaining momentum. Stiegler (2011: 4) refers to 'a new critique' calling for 'a philosophical leap, an exit from the dogmatic slumbers that have accumulated in the twentieth century in philosophy, but also in science'. The implication of this is the following: 'it must be an analysis of the limits of the object of critique, and the *elaboration of a renewed idea of this object*' (my italics). In other words: think new, think differently, think inventively.

Since Husserl, many more recent thinkers and scientists have expressed concerns about the sciences in general. Emphasis is laid on negative outcomes that have detrimental impacts on individuals and communities and, even wider, on the world/earth. This occurs despite the many positive achievements which cannot and should never be denied. David Bohm, a well-renowned physicist, while admitting the achievements, clearly expresses the urgency of thinking of science and its meaning in new and different terms (in Bohm & Peat, 1989). In an interview Bohm (in Bohm & Peat, 1989: 1–14) makes it clear that a new thinking about the sciences and what science means is imperative: 'We have to explore in a creative way what a new notion of science might be, a notion that is suitable for our present time. This means that all the subjects that we have been talking about will have to come into the discussion' (in Bohm & Peat, 1989: 14). In answer to the statement by his partner in conversation, David Peat, Bohm states: 'We are beginning to realize that the cost of progress is more and more specialization and fragmentation to the point where the whole activity is losing its meaning. I think that the time has come for science to pause and take a careful look at where it is going' (Bohm & Peat, 1989: 11). Bohm answered: 'I think that even more than this we need to change what we mean by "science". The moment has come for a creative surge along new lines' (Bohm & Peat, 1989: 11). This does not mean the denial of the meaning of science as it is generally pursued. Bohm continues:

> *Of course, a century ago the benefits from science generally outweighed the negative effects, even when the whole endeavour was carried out without regard for long-range consequences. But the modern world is finite and we have almost unlimited powers of destruction. It is clear that the world has passed a point of no return. This is one reason why we have to pause and consider the possibility of a fundamental and extensive change in what science means to us.*
>
> *(Bohm & Peat, 1989: 13).*

This reminds us once again of 'the crisis of the sciences' Husserl had in mind.

Examples of how to direct our rethinking of the sciences include *The Uncertain Quest* (Salomon, Sagasti, & Sachs-Jeantet, 1994), 'Mode 2 knowledge' as developed by Gibbons et al. (1994) in their book, *The New Production of Knowledge*, *Re-Thinking Science* (Nowotny, Scott, & Gibbons, 2004) and the latest book by Isabelle Stengers (2013), *Une autre science est possible!* These different groups of authors leave us in no uncertainty about the necessary and promising possibilities of the rethinking of the sciences, but above all about our responsibility. This has to be taken up with a view to promising meaningful outcomes. Such a rethinking implies, on the one hand, the questioning of the fixities, certainties and determinacies of the accepted views and convictions like the end of certainty (Prigogine, 1997), and on the other hand the suggestion of alternatives, that is 'the new scientific spirit' of Gaston Bachelard (1985), and the postmodern view of knowledge (Lyotard, 1995). What boggles the mind is that these formidable examples exist but are steadfastly ignored. We should never forget the important fact that information work has a responsibility to gather and distribute information, including information related to and regarding science, its dimensions, its status, its limitations, its achievements and its different perspectives. We should be on top of developments relating to the scientific endeavour in its widest and deepest possible sense. The failure of science regarding meaning and total existence is a failure of information science and information work regarding responsible informational engagement with the sciences. We have a responsibility to bring forward as many views as possible on 'the best possible science' (see Roux & De Beer, 2011 in this regard).

Bachelard's 'new scientific spirit' assumes the existence of an old and outdated scientific spirit. This suggests that it is possible and necessary to work towards an alternative. Lyotard also indicates in what direction we should be moving in our critique and in our search for an alternative view of science. His suggestion that we should move away from the deterministic tendency in scientific work, as mentioned earlier, towards a situation where complexity, dynamics and uncertainty are also taken seriously would indeed require 'a new scientific spirit' in terms of which the paradoxes that can be expected can be addressed. For Lyotard the accepted principle that systems, physical systems and even social systems, follow regular patterns as suggested above is fiction. The newness lies in the fact that quantum mechanics and atomic physics 'require a radical revision of the idea of a continuous and predictable path' (Lyotard, 1995: 167). The problem is that any measurement becomes problematic as indicated by the mathematician Mandelbrot in his theory of fractals. Another mathematician, René Thom, emphasises that 'discontinuities can occur in determined phenomena, causing them to take unexpected forms: this constitutes what is known as catastrophe theory' (Lyotard, 1995: 169). In this way determinism, predictability and certainty are turned upside down. Disciplinary research, as it is currently understood and pursued, is losing its pre-eminence as a paradigm of knowledge and prediction, and requires new and different articulations of reality and humans and their relationship to that which is in totality. This brings us close to the possibility of claiming a post-scientific position for information science. To put it in the words of Lyotard:

*Postmodern science — by concerning itself by such things as undecidables, the limits of precise control, conflicts characterised by incomplete information, 'fractal', catastrophes and pragmatic paradoxes — is theorizing its own evolution as discontinuous, catastrophic, non-rectifiable, and paradoxical. It is changing the meaning of the word knowledge, while expressing how such a change can take place. It is producing not the known but the unknown. And it suggests a model of legitimation*

*that has nothing to do with maximized performance, but has as its basic difference*
*understood as paralogy. (1995: 170)*

The suggestion of paralogy is that new offensives are required in the new scientific spirit that will also enable information science to move in the direction of the new scientific spirit, to use Bachelard's terminology. Lyotard wants to bring back narrative in all the discourses of legitimation − the scientists (but also knowledge workers, I wish to add) are before anything else people who tell stories. The emphasis here is on generating ideas, the imaginative invention of solutions to the diversity of problems, the going beyond methods, that is paralogy in the true sense (see Kent, 1993). The imaginative development of knowledge should be our main aim. A little story can often do the trick. 'Paralogy is more than and different from innovation. Innovation is under command of the system, of sameness. Paralogy goes beyond the system and the same, beyond consensus, towards dissention, towards difference. In this sense it is morphogenetic (Thom)' (Lyotard, 1995: 171).

The problem is whether it is possible to have an approach that will still be legitimate when based solely on paralogy. Could we contemplate this as an option for our field? According to Lyotard it is a vibrant option indeed:

*Dissention ... must be emphasized. Consensus is a horizon that is never reached.*
*Research that takes place under the aegis of a paradigm tends to stabilize; it is like*
*the exploitation of a technological, economic, artistic 'idea'. It cannot be dis-*
*counted. But what is striking is that someone always comes along to disturb the*
*order of 'reason'. (1995: 171)*

A distinction is made by Deleuze and Guattari (1987) between 'nomad or ambulant sciences' and 'royal sciences' where 'royal sciences' represent science in its more or less standardised form and 'nomad sciences' represent something altogether different and new in emphasis as well as direction. This splendid differentiation gives us another opening to a different way of thinking about science. (See Chapter 2 for the initial discussion of this distinction and the emphasis to which this paragraph is simply complementary.) The characterisation of this differentiation by Isabelle Stengers (2000: 156−7) opens one's eyes to something excitingly new in the field of scientific work. While the royal sciences transform problems to fit into their frameworks, schemes and procedures, the ambulant or nomad sciences view problems in their full context and with this in mind the solutions must be supple, collective and comprehensive. This comes close to the suggestion in these chapters of a post-scientific position for science, but also and especially for information science. The royal sciences designate an available world or an identified problem, and work towards its objective reduction to something manageable that can be controlled, subjected and manipulated. In the context of a post-scientific approach the scientific vocation would not be to reduce the multiplicity of sensible phenomena to a manageable unity but to construct the intelligibility of their qualitative difference. In this regard understanding means to create a language that opens up the possibility of encountering different sensible forms without subjecting them to control or manipulating them. The ambulant sciences celebrate a story, they actualise new existents through multiple metamorphoses and the addition of ever new significations in ever-new milieus. It seems as if this brief description of the ambulant or nomad sciences provides an intelligible model for the scientific endeavour to follow, but even more so an excellent model for information science.

These views of Lyotard, inspired by Bachelard and strengthened by the views of Deleuze and Guattari, are complemented and reinforced by many thinkers and scientists from a broad spectrum of intellectual and scientific involvement. (See Atlan (1986), Ekeland (1988), Bohm and Peat (1989), Bohm (2009), Gibbons et al. (1994), Salomon et al. (1994), Prigogine (1997), Stengers (2000) and Nowotny et al. (2004) as a few pertinent examples with a high standing in this regard — there are many others who could be mentioned.) These thinkers radically question the traditional or classical conception of science as maintained in terms of 'scientific realism'.

The rethinking that is at issue here is an endeavour to bring science closer to reality in its fullness, but especially closer to human reality, human meaning and 'total existence', as Husserl suggested. A concise summary of the views emerging from the above-mentioned leading theoreticians and thinkers in this endeavour may be useful. When Henri Atlan uses crystal and smoke, Ekeland uses calculation and the unforeseen, Hayles (2005) pattern and randomness, and Prigogine and Stengers determinism and indeterminism, the real challenge is not to see these conceptual pairs as opposites but as complementary. These complementary pairs are conceptualisations of reality, including human reality, in its fullness. These are complementary ways of articulating the real of which certain aspects are certain while other aspects are less certain or clear. It can be neatly summarised by way of a statement by Atlan:

> It is here that the two opposing notions of repetition, regularity, and redundancy on the one hand, and variety, improbability, and complexity on the other, can be recognized as coexistent in dynamic organisations. What is encountered here is a compromise between two extremes: a repetitive, perfectly symmetric order of which the crystal is the most classical physical model, and a variety, infinitely complex in its details, like the evanescent forms of smoke. (1986: 5, my translation)

Atlan finds a strong ally in Ekeland who states:

> We turn our backs to the world we belong to ... We cannot gain a direct understanding of reality ... Our gaze is turned to the stream of time — or rather to that small stretch of its flow by which we sit and which we call the present. This contemplation is science itself. It creates strange monsters, which invade the whole world and eventually turn against us. (1988: 121)

The standardised scientific position is to focus on the first only to the neglect of the second, and in so doing science reduces reality to something less and becomes itself reduced to research and as such highly impoverished. The post-scientific position is to accept full responsibility for thinking these seemingly opposing parts of the real together in their complementary unity. But they are even more than that in the sense that they are interdependent — the one cannot be understood or even granted existence without the other. To take only one into consideration means to be highly reductionistic and, as Bohm (2009: 127) correctly indicates, the implication of this is always 'destructive' and has 'bad effects'. Only compositional thinking can articulate reality irreductionistic and in its fullness. In order to articulate this 'fullness of reality' requires a kind of comprehensive thinking, here called compositional thinking, and this is the only way by which the 'crisis of the sciences' (Husserl), the 'destruction', the 'bad effects' (Bohm, 2009), the possible 'catastrophic outcomes'(Stengers, 2009) and 'barbaric consequences' (Henry, 2012) of reductionism can be avoided or eliminated. This is valid for the sciences in general but more specifically is also very pertinent for information science in particular. The rethinking is not only necessary for the sake of accuracy and completeness, but more specifically from the perspective of a moral obligation.

## 3.5  Conclusion

Against this background, if we want a truly responsible engagement with science, we are forced to rethink science and to start thinking about science in a new way while realising the decisive importance of encountering a new kind of science as well as with respect to the exciting new opportunities such a rethinking provides. Maybe this is something of what the physicist Bohm anticipated in his book with the significant title *Science, Order and Creativity*. This is a book that everyone with a real scientific interest should read and digest, together with his other book, *On Creativity*, especially the interview and the preface. A suitable other name, if we want to take Bohm seriously and I think we should, may be to start with what can be called a 'post-science' or a 'post-scientific' perspective or position for the scientific endeavour, to lean on Lyotard's perspective of the 'postmodern'. It should be kept in mind that the term 'postmodern' does not in the first place mean to be 'post' in the chronological sense, but more in a qualitative sense, the sense of 'beyond'. Postmodern does not refer to what comes after modern, but is more in terms of a-modern which can refer to both pre- and after modern but also even to intra-modern. Another example of such a new term that may be considered as more adequate can be found in the distinction made by Deleuze and Guattari (1987) between 'nomad sciences' and 'royal sciences' where 'royal sciences' represent science in its more or less standardised form and the 'nomad sciences' represent something altogether different and new in emphasis as well as direction. Nomad science in the sense of science on the move, a science that crosses boundaries, may be particularly useful for and a significant pointer to information science which is constantly in a situation of crossing boundaries, especially conceptual boundaries and disciplinary boundaries, entering into and exploring new and different domains of knowledge with a view to sensible practices. In Chapter 4 this alternative, and what it requires from the perspective of information science, will be dealt with. It may be significant to mention that Bachelard (1983) devotes a book to 'the formation of the scientific spirit' in order to promote the new scientific spirit as articulated here.

# References

Atlan, H. (1986). *Entre le cristal et la fumée*. Paris: Seuil.

Bachelard, G. (1983). *La formation de l'esprit scientifique*. Paris: Vrin.

Bachelard, G. (1985). *The new scientific spirit*. New York: Beacon Press.

Ballay, J. (2010) *Le mythe de l'intelligence collective*. Online at: <http://arsindustrialis.org/le-mythe-de-lintelligence-collective-0> Accessed 25.10.10.

Bohm, D. (2009). *On creativity*. London: Routledge Classics.

Bohm, D., & Peat, F. D. (1989). *Science, order and creativity*. London: Routledge.

Bougnoux, D. (1995). Qui a peur de l'information? In R. Capurro, K. Wiegerling, & A. Brellochs (Eds.), *Informationsethik*. Konstanz: Universitätsverlag.

Buckland, M. (2011). What kind of science can information science be? *Journal of the American Society for Information Science and Technology, 63*(1), 1−7.

Cronin, B. (1995). Shibboleth and substance in North American library and information science education. *Libri, 45*, 45−63.

Day, R. E. (2004). Poststructuralism and information studies. In B. Cronin (Ed.), *Annual review of information science and technology* (pp. 575−609). Medford, NJ: Information Today.

Day, R. E. (2008). *The modern invention of information: Discourse, history, and power*. Carbondale, IL: Southern Illinois University Press.

De Beer, C. S. (2011). Methodology and noology: Amazing prospects for library and information science. *South African Journal for Library and Information Science, 77*(1), 85−92.

Deleuze, G., & Guattari, F. (1987). *A thousand plateaus: Capitalism and schizophrenia*. Minneapolis, MN: Minnesota University Press.

Ekeland, I. (1988). *Mathematics and the unexpected*. Chicago: University of Chicago Press.

Frohmann, B. (1994). Communication technologies and the politics of postmodern information science. *Canadian Journal for Information and Library Science, 19*(2), 1−22.

Gibbons, M., Limoges, C., Nowotny, H., Schwarzman, Z., Scott, P., & Trow, M. (1994). *The new production of knowledge: The dynamics of science in contemporary societies*. London: Sage.

Hayles, K. N. (2005). *My mother was a computer: Digital subjects and literary texts*. Chicago: University of Chicago Press.

Henry, M. (2012). *Barbarism*. London: Continuum.

Husserl, E. (1970). *The crisis of European sciences and transcendental phenomenology*. Evanston, IL: Northwestern University Press.

Kent, T. (1993). *A theory of communicative interaction*. Lewisburg, PA: Bucknell University Press.

Laszlo, E. (1989). *The inner limits of mankind*. London: Oneworld.

Lyotard, J.-F. (1995). The contemporary pragmatics of scientific knowledge. In J. D. Faubion (Ed.), *Rethinking the subject*. Boulder, CO: Westview Press.

Midgley, M. (1991). *Wisdom, information and wonder: What is knowledge for?* London: Routledge.

Morin, E. (1990). *Science avec conscience*. Paris: Seuil.

Nowotny, H., Scott, P., & Gibbons, M. (2004). *Re-thinking science: Knowledge and the public in an age of uncertainty* (5th ed.). Cambridge: Polity Press.

Prigogine, I. (1997). *The end of certainty: Time, chaos and the new laws of nature*. New York: Free Press.

Roux, A. P. J., & De Beer, C. S. (2010a). Onderweg na goeie wetenskap 1: Ewekniebeoordeling: Betroubare weegskaal of vyfde wiel aan die wa? *LitNet Akademies*, *7*(2), 129–164. Online at: <http://www.oulitnet.co.za/akademiesgeestes/pdf/LA72debeer.pdf>.

Roux, A. P. J., & De Beer, C. S. (2010b). Onderweg na goeie wetenskap 2: Die funksie van strategie, visie en beleid. *LitNet Akademies*, *7*(3), 323–381. Online at: <http://www.oulitnet.co.za/akademiesgeestes/pdf/LA73debeerroux.pdf>.

Roux, A. P. J., & De Beer, C. S. (2011). Onderweg na goeie wetenskap 3: Voorwaardes vir die beste moontlike wetenskap. *LitNet Akademies*, *8*(3), 242–278 Online at: <http://www.litnet.co.za/assets/pdf/9Roux%20en%20De%20Beer.pdf>.

Salomon, J.-J., Sagasti, F. R., & Sachs-Jeantet, C. (1994). *The uncertain quest: Science, technology, and development*. Tokyo: United Nations University Press.

Stengers, I. (2000). *The invention of modern science*. Minneapolis, MN: University of Minnesota Press.

Stengers, I. (2009). *Au temps des catastrophes: Résister à la barbarie qui vient. Paris*. La Découverte.

Stengers, I. (2013). *Une autre science est possible! Manifeste pour un ralentissement de sciences. Paris*. La Découverte.

Stiegler, B. (2011). *Disbelief and discredit*, (Vol. 1)*, the decadence of industrial democracies*. Cambridge: Polity Press.

Virilio, P. (2000). *The information bomb*. London: Verso.

Warner, J. (2001). W(h)ither information science?/!. *Library Quarterly*, *71*(2), 243–255.

Wersig, G. (1990). The changing role of knowledge in an information society. In D. J. Foskett (Ed.), *The information environment: A world view*. New York: Elsevier Science.

Wersig, G. (1993a). *Fokus Mensch: Bezugspunkte postmoderner Wissenschaft: Wissen, Kommunikation, Kultur*. Frankfurt am Main: Peter Lang.

Wersig, G. (1993b). Information science: The study of postmodern knowledge usage. *Information Processing and Management*, *29*(2), 229–239.

# Information science in a post-scientific position

**4**

## Part 2: The conditions for an alternative

### 4.1 Introduction

The alternative that should be considered, as suggested in the previous chapter, is that instead of reducing the real which is the 'safer' option and for which we are schooled, the option should be taken to expand ourselves, not only our means (especially the technical means), but ourselves, in terms of the expansion of our given capacities: instead of settling for the degree zero of thought the maximising of our thinking capacity should be explored. This would imply the cultivation of a capacity to deal with reality as such in its unreduced state, with a firm unwillingness to reduce. Hereby imagination, phantasy and dreamery or reverie must be creatively and inventively included. In his most recent book Stiegler (2013: 326−68) confirms this need for the cultivation of capacity and is explicit about the urgency of the issue of what he calls 'recapacitation', and that is exactly what is suggested to be pursued here in our context. The capacity for knowledge and thinking that was lost during the course of time must be rebuilt. It is most definitely not merely a matter of developing skills, but a matter of adopting a newly invented set of conceptual equipment, or rather capabilities.

In an age of multi-, inter- and trans-disciplinarity we can no longer afford to take the reductive, dogmatising route of locking up knowledge within strictly demarcated boundaries. As a matter of fact we have to move, and to move fast, in the opposite direction. We are challenged in many ways to acknowledge the *multiple* nature of reality (we have to expand our view of the real as well) and the essential urgency to *connect* and relate as many as possible matters from as many as possible sources in order to achieve, find or invent answers, directions, solutions for human individuals and societies, and this must be done in a *thoughtful* way for our inventions to succeed: multiple, connective intellection (Serres, 1980, 1995, 2009).

'The complex set of newly developing approaches', as suggested by Gernot Wersig, fits in here in a perfect way. The emphasis is on conceptualisation and intellectual input. There is no other way in which this can be done. The moment we start thinking about need, about solutions, serious thinking must be done. It is

Information Science as an Interscience.

unavoidable. There is always thinking involved when meaning is the issue. As our knowledge, our sciences, our disciplines become more and more connected and linked all measures of self-protection, self-preservation, safe cities, even narcissistic self-deception – my occupied place is the only place to be – and narcissistic sciences and disciplines are manifestly nothing but arrogant and infantile. The fixed conception of knowledge offers nothing exciting, nothing adventurous, nothing lively and vibrating, but only boring, deadening, disturbing, debilitated fragments of nothingness that need to be repeated constantly.

This is where the rich insights on 'irreduction' by Latour (1988: 153–236, especially pp. 212–36 on the 'irreduction' of the sciences), the refusal to reduce anything, even reality itself, to less than what it is come into play. In view of 'irreduction' he asks the significant questions:

> *What happens when nothing is reduced to nothing else? What happens when we suspend our knowledge of what a force is? What happens when we do not know how their way of relating to one another is changing? What happens when we give up this burden, this passion, this indignation, this obsession, this flame, this fury, this dazzling aim, this excess, this insane desire to reduce everything?'*
>
> *(Latour, 1988: 157)*

The implication is that we have to refuse to think in terms of binary oppositions in which we reduce one of the oppositional members to only one of the two opposites. We must rather accept the challenge to think the opposite extremes together, to compose them into a complementary totality, into a well-integrated web of significance and signification. Examples, as discussed in the previous chapter, of these extremes as they emerge in a scientific context are the following: crystal and smoke (Atlan); the measurable and the immeasurable (Bernardis and Hagene); pattern and randomness (Hayles); chance and necessity (Monod); determinism and indeterminism (Prigogine and Stengers); etc. With this in mind the 'multiple, connective intellection' of Michel Serres and compositional, transductional thinking of Bernard Stiegler are making an enormous amount of sense and should be pursued. Transduction wants to say that complementary terms are not merely complementary but the one is the constitutive condition for the other. They must always be thought together to avoid fatal impoverishment. Information science as an interscience has already been suggested as highly suitable in an exemplary way for this kind of transductional thinking. In this way reality will not deliberately and strategically be impoverished but its richness will be encountered and embraced and the insights of scientists such as Atlan, Monod, Ekeland, Prigogine and others will at last be understood with their full implications. Some more about these views has been articulated in the previous chapter. It will also bring us closer to the notion of complexity as a vital way of articulating reality as it has been articulated in many ways by Edgar Morin (1990), but also by Gernot Wersig from a direct information science perspective (see Wersig, 1995). The emphasis on these scientific and theoretical developments has unlocked new avenues for information science to be rethought with a view to a new role in individual and societal contexts.

## 4.2    Alternative offered to information science in terms of this other conception of science

It is clear from Chapter 3 that information science cannot really be at home in the company of the sciences as currently defined. Its position should therefore urgently be reconsidered. There is more than one scientific approach and conception of science. There is the generally accepted notion of science: closed disciplines, rigid and explicit methods and clearly defined objects. None of these is true or can possibly be true of information science and its domain of work, although we try very hard to comply with these requirements and try to force a place open for ourselves. It cannot happen and will never happen. We have to explore other options. We have to accept that the generally accepted idea of science is not the only idea of science and certainly not for us. There are fully legitimate alternatives where in a much more comfortable and a much more significant and fruitful way we may fit in!

The proposal in this contribution is that we should take up a post-scientific position for information science, as suggested in Chapter 3, in the sense of the postmodern condition of knowledge (Lyotard), as it has already been explored to some significant extent by Wersig (1990, 1992, 1993a, 1993b), Frohmann (1994), Day (2004, 2008) and others in our subject field, and in the spirit of the 'multiple connective intellection', which is also acritical, according to the views of Michel Serres. The idea of a nomad science with an emphasis on nomad activities in the sense of moving between disciplines and between the multiple dimensions of the real, as articulated by Deleuze and Guattari (1987), could add some significant insights to this whole effort. Attention to the theory of plasticity (in its shaping, form-giving, as well as the form-destructing aspects) as developed by Catherine Malabou (2008, 2010), and as it may be made applicable to in-form-ation activities, may bear rich fruit. The whole endeavour should be pursued in the spirit of Bachelard's 'new scientific spirit' and his suggestions about 'the formation of the scientific spirit' along the same lines as suggested in Chapter 3.

In the process this suggested option does not become less scientific but rather much more responsibly scientific. Moving away from the classical idea of the sciences as disciplines with demarcated areas and methods that give access and entrance to these areas, which are in any event becoming outdated in view of inter-, multi- and transdisciplinarities, should be high on the agenda. Knowledge is now the issue and 'information as knowledge for action' is the issue par excellence (see Kuhlen, 2004, and Wersig, 1992, in this regard). It becomes more scientific in the sense of more knowledgeable. Perhaps we should get back to knowledge as an activity, knowledge as it is reflected as activity, in the Latin verb *scire* and the Greek verb for knowing *gignwskein*. In both cases the emphasis is on knowing, the act of knowing. 'Information is knowledge for action' (Wersig and Kuhlen). Maintaining or regaining the action position brings it in line with the history of science. While the 'pre-scientific' period was a period during which knowledge activities were present but not yet referred to as science in the contemporary sense, it was science in another sense but certainly not less than science. The post-scientific position as proposed here is also a move beyond the sciences, away from their standard strategies and closer to reality (both natural and human) in its fullness. This move poses serious and deeply challenging demands.

We have superb examples in the figures of Bougnoux, Cronin, Day, Frohmann and Wersig who actively and fruitfully pursue this possibility and who need our attention and even following. A brief summary of how they resist the temptation of associating themselves with the standard approaches and what they offer as an alternative, not only regarding a view of information science on the one hand, but especially also views about the intellectual challenges and how and in terms of what to face them may be very enlightening. Bougnoux introduces the notion of interscience; Cronin puts emphasis on information access; Day highlights the power of documents as social and historical forces that construct imaginations (fantasies); Frohmann develops the idea of information power; Wersig leans strongly towards the effectiveness of interconcepts and this links up marvellously with the ideas of Bougnoux and the idea of an interscience.

Daniel Bougnoux (1993) proposes the fruitful and very significant idea of an interdiscipline or an interscience. This idea was explored in the South African context a few years ago as a fruitful and significant development worth pursuing, but stays unfortunately without any significant response (see De Beer, 2005). What is especially interesting is the fact that Stiegler (2012: 279–355), in a very recent publication in the context of the status of the contemporary university, gives special attention to the idea of an interscience even in a wider and more general context than information science, as an unavoidable and highly important contemporary development. He strongly recommends that 'an interscience for the 21st century must take form in the heart of the universities of the entire world' (Stiegler, 2012: 301–2). This should encourage us to pursue this matter further in a much more definitive and substantial sense. Information science can become a superb example of how this exciting initiative can be effectuated.

Bougnoux's emphasis on an interscience links up with Wersig's idea, namely 'interconcepts'. Bougnoux is a formidable theoretician in the field of information and communication sciences with a very specific emphasis on the idea of an interscience or interdiscipline. He demonstrates to what extent information science is a science between the sciences, that this is its strong point and cannot be otherwise. It contradicts the recent statement by Buckland (2011) that the 'inter' of interscience is its weak point. Quite the contrary. The weak points in the sciences are all the points where a specific object is focused on while its contexts and relations with other objects are ignored. Consequently the objectivistic attitude of the sciences is their capacity to distort; this also has its pathological implications and therefore this objectivistic attitude is not necessarily their strong point. Reductions are terrorism (Badiou).

The significance of Bougnoux for our purposes is the fact that he positively establishes relationships between information science and philosophy, semiotics, speech acts and language, a theory of the masses, the dangerous and very machination of thought, and a focus on community recovery or reinvention. When we look at these disciplinary sciences closely we immediately realise that it is of central importance for information science to explore and utilise these connections to the full. Bougnoux calls for extensive intellectual activity. An intermediary space is called for in view of any informational or semiotic relationship while a stimulus-response or cause-effect relationship puts us on the edge of the grave. To the 'intermediary space which is called for in view of any informational or semiotic relationship', Bougnoux (1995: 77) adds: 'Information has the strange quality of existing only between order and pure disorder, between the closure of the crystal and the openness of smoke, and that it demands a zest of communication or a relation that can be altogether deadly. Information is a study of the force of words or of symbolic effectiveness.'

Note the strong emphasis on the fertility of the 'between' or the 'inter'. He further emphasises that 'rigid or crystallised thinking in the context of information science and work does not contribute to information just as amorphous thought cannot make any contribution either. Information dies by the excess of closedness as well as by the excess of openness and lives by the compromise between these two extreme pitfalls of crystal and smoke' (Bougnoux, 1995: 75; see also Atlan, 1986).

Cronin (1995: 56) makes valuable suggestions as to what the real focus of information science should be as an answer to the question he himself posed: 'What constitutes the underpinning of our hybrid field?' (Cronin, 1995: 56). He emphasises the importance of 'the idea of disciplinary interaction combined with conceptual outsourcing' and in a direct sense links this with what he calls 'Wersig's enlightened view of information science as a new or postmodern science' and his plea for 'the idea of inter-concepts' (see Wersig, 1992 and 1993b, on this). The prominence of intellectual underpinnings, conceptual interchanges and disciplinary interactions as fundamentally important foci for information science and work should be embraced. Cronin goes even further by emphasising that 'a more productive approach may be to ask what is the absolute, irreducible essence of our field ... that both defines what we do in a fundamental sense and differentiates us ... from all other academic tribes' (Cronin, 1995: 58). An answer to this might be 'information access', a highly elastic term that connotes intellectual, physical, social, economic and spatial/temporal access (Cronin, 1995: 58). Albeit the case that these components are all valuable, they are unfortunately inadequate, and in more than one respect quite problematic, unless more comprehensively interpreted and complemented than is normally the case.

Frohmann (1994: 17) suggests that 'a theoretical shift to information power challenges information science to confront its own politics of interpretation of its keywords − "information systems", "information needs", "information users" and "information uses" − which currently belong to discourses constructing communication and information technologies according to prevailing inequities of power over information'. This politics of interpretation is in line with the 'standard conception of science' from which it is urgent to move away, especially if we want to achieve meaning. According to him 'information power' is the key − needs, uses and users should be replaced with information power (Frohmann, 1994: 2). The interpretation of information power is important here. It opens the road to proper 'informatisation' as the activity that is giving shape and form. The idea of 'information power' may be risky and even dangerous, especially when the work of Michel

Foucault on the analyses of power is kept in mind. Of course, information, when well-defined, constitutes a force that can shape and change lives and societies. When this idea is combined with Malabou's theory of plasticity the full significance of information in its deep relationship with knowledge will unfold as the deepest meaning-giving entity in the human world. The three aspects of the theory of plasticity relevant for us are the form-giving, the form-undergoing and the form-destructing aspects. This is exactly what in-form-ation in its true sense is all about, and that emphasises its workings in society and in human life and offers a focus for both information science and information work.

From a poststructural perspective Day (2004) comes forward with some very pertinent perspectives of decisive value to us in this consideration of thinking differently about information science and its foci. He writes about the poststructural view that:

> *It aims at destroying the metaphysical assumptions of positivism and bringing into question the ... contemporary notions of knowledge, information and popular notions of language. It thus opens up other, older understandings of knowledge, information, and language, such as those based on affects and events (see Wersig, 1990 and 1993a). This reopening of language to something other than auto-affective meaning or data, this reopening of knowledge to something other than certain mental contents and this reopening of information to something other than representation, fact or 'true belief', constitute a challenge to the metaphysical and epistemological assumptions that have, for so long, dominated not only information studies research and even practice, but also popular conceptions of the materials it studies.*
>
> *(Day, 2004: 581)*

This is as strong an argument for the rethinking of information science and its subdisciplines as one can possibly get. The radical rethinking of knowledge, information and language implies the rethinking of the essence of the subject field. The rethinking presupposes a different way of thinking and of the highly demanded conceptual equipment for this purpose. The available, generally utilised conceptual equipment is totally inadequate because it is too limited and short-sighted to envisage anything outside the boundaries of the prescribed routes. What is needed is to move 'off the beaten track' as the condition for reinventing information science itself, all its core notions and, of course, every single subdiscipline. In addition to Day's own observations and insights we can benefit a great deal from Wersig, Kuhlen and Stiegler in the rethinking not only of knowledge and information but also the rethinking of their link to language, from Lecercle (1990) and Blair (2006). This rethinking, if pursued extensively, honestly and responsibly, will self-evidently put information science on a new exciting basis from where both its theory and its practice can be enriched.

Wersig (1993a: 233–4) remarks: 'Information science is not a discipline in the classical sense of the sciences, but belongs to a complex set of newly developing approaches.' He elaborates on this statement in a special chapter in his *Fokus Mensch* with the title 'Der Weg in eine neue Wissenschaftlichkeit' ('Road into a

New Scientificness') (Wersig, 1993a: 129–67). He articulates in an excellent way a post-scientific position for information science and emphasises at the same time that

> *classical scientificness has its boundaries or limitations; that other forms of scienti-*
> *ficness need to be carefully attended to; and that the programme suggested in this*
> *study, when viewed from the perspective of knowing (that is in a direct sense to be*
> *related to categories of meaning, lifestyle, and education) belongs to the context of*
> *this new scientificness.*
>
> *(Wersig, 1993a: 129)*

Equally important for the future, and related to this, is Wersig's (1990, 1993a) plea that we should understand the actors in the information environment if we want to renew information science. We have to focus on the human being as still the most important actor and not on information and communication technologies, and then, of course, human action is not the same as human behaviour – there is a vital difference.

In addition to this and with an emphasis on the societal dimension of human actors Warner (2001: 252) formulates the challenge to information science as follows: 'to broaden its academic remit to include serious consideration of the "information society" and how it interlocks with the total social situation'. This emphasises exactly my argument that only when a post-scientific position is accepted for information science will information scientists and information workers focus on what they are in the last analysis supposed to be focusing on, namely meaning, lifestyle and total human existence – in other words on the societal dimension in an explicit way. In this regard a deep rethinking of the sociality, namely the socius of society, is desperately needed (De Beer, 2010). The condition for this, however, is that we realise the limitations of 'classical science' and open our eyes and minds for other forms of scientificness besides this classical form. Considering these views and statements an alternative conception of science for information science unfolds.

There are certainly more examples but these are the most explicit, well-articulated and properly substantiated views. We have in other words strong arguments from philosophico-theoretical perspectives as well as from the perspective of scientific and knowledge dynamics and the perspective of technical developments that all of them work towards the breakdown of the classical divide between subject and object, and the problems of the fixity of the real and of method. It has never been made manifest regarding its implications for scientific work. Perhaps this is the time to pursue precisely this and maybe information science can offer a superb example of how this can and should be done.

Information science, as discussed here, is a science without an object like the other sciences, and consequently without a method like the other disciplines. The redefinition of information science implies not only the redefinition of all the sub-disciplines mentioned earlier, but more than that: not only objects but reality needs to be redefined, the human being as central actor in the information world needs to be drastically rearticulated (see Wersig, 1990 and 1993a), and the methodical approach in its total poverty needs to be completely rethought (see De Beer, 2011).

In the process of thinking differently about object, subject and method another dynamics must be put in place and acted upon. We have to realise that objects are multi-faceted and multi-connected, are very often inserted between disciplines and are dynamic and not static, and we must therefore be able to think across disciplines and even beyond an accepted notion of truth as generally defined in the context of the disciplines. And method needs to be replaced by compositional thinking eager to deal with the multiple facets of relevant knowledges often to be combined and articulated with a view to complex problem situations. Our methods often blur our vision and block our view. The newly defined information science and its redefined subdisciplines will be able to dare to tackle complex situations rather than try to simplify everything. As part of its redefined stature it will not hesitate to confront and encounter the complex for the sake of meaning and sense-making. This was well articulated by Fernandes and Kobashi (2010) who make significant points in this regard, especially with a view to the place of the notion of complexity in information science. That makes it impossible to treat information and knowledge any longer in a representational style.

The implication is that the *subject* can no longer be interpreted as fixed, static, rational and individualistic but must be rethought as a multiple, supple, communal and noological or spiritual being that is thoughtfully open to everything. The *object* loses its character as present, limited, without context and reified. When the object becomes thought it becomes affected by other objects, constituting a world of inter-connectedness, and by an ecology that determines its meaning and exposes it as containing unexpected, unforeseen, unpredictable, immeasurable, uncertain and random dimensions to it. *Method* will be exchanged for thought, not one-dimensional and linear, but compositional, comprehensive, reflective and multiple, in order to really penetrate the world and multiple reality from one side to the other and to articulate what it encounters in terms of meaning. Real problem-solving will only come to its right in such situations.

These redefined issues have a deeply significant impact on our subject-field and all its subdisciplines, their definition, functioning and impact. In this way information science can become what it is meant to be, namely a theoretical as well as practical endeavour to shape the world, human lives, societal situations and dynamics towards the realisation of meaning. In this regard it may be useful to take a close and constant look at what is called 'epistemo-critique' (*SubStance*, 1993) as the breaking down of disciplinary boundaries, the continuous rethinking of knowledge in its dynamic dimensions, and the encouragement of the flow of knowledges to wherever they may be needed and may take us. This is exactly the intention with this chapter and book.

In the new knowledge age (De Beer, 2009) the demands and challenges posed to information science are enormous. The danger is to hide or run away from the challenges by locking ourselves up in well-protected, so-called safe niches. This normally entails a matter of reductive strategies, denying the challenges or taking what we may consider to be dogmatic stands. Such an approach misses the real possibility of finding real solutions to real problems and for this very reason the invention of a new set of conceptual equipment should be pursued.

# 4.3 A newly invented set of conceptual equipment should be proposed

In order to give expression to the rethinking of information science in an adequate way it is of vital importance to us to become aware of the scope and the comprehensive impact of information and information-related issues on individuals and society which will in a self-evident way show the necessity for a clear understanding of the limitations of 'standard' and 'standardised' approaches to the scientific endeavour and for the invention of an adequate conceptual equipment.

## 4.3.1 The massive, but also disturbing, impact of information/ knowledge on and in society

This is well-illustrated by Midgley (1991), Virilio (2000), Lash (2002), Poster (2006), Gleick (2012) and many others. Given these studies on the scope and impact that exposed the complexity of matters regarding information and the idea of an information society, which can be referred to as the 'information explosion' that may cause 'information anxiety' (Wurman, 1991) on a wide scale, much more is needed than the mere traditional information science approach to these matters since it will most definitely fall short in terms of capacity. This 'information explosion' should be pursued and understood in the light of the rethinking of information science as suggested in the previous section which articulates different approaches and strategies for sense-making in this new and very dynamic context.

Gleick (2012) emphasises in his epilogue, under the subheading 'The Return of Meaning', that 'It was inevitable that meaning would force its way back' (a quote from the formidable study of Dupuy, *The Mechanization of the Mind* (2000). Here we encounter the real challenge confronting the information scientist: move away from pleasing politicians, stay away from quasi-scientific escapades, restrain yourselves from the obsession with the criticisms of the day. There is another need: the need for meaning. Does life, my life, your life, the life of your client make sense? That is ultimately what the question should be about. That is what informatisation is all about: let us make, shape meaning wherever we are and in whatever we do. Going back to Husserl's crisis and the contemplation of a positive response to it. Information science has a responsibility to deal with this crisis for its own sake; it is a vital part of its *raison d'être* (its reason to be).

When one reads the views of Scott Lash (2002) on the information society one finds quite a different perspective. According to him meaning is no longer the issue. Communication operationality is what matters in this context. His effort to turn things upside down and to reorganise all used and usable terminology requires thorough and fundamental thinking. It is challenging and we should not fail to respond. A response calls, however, for a different conceptualisation, at least away from operationalisation as the new 'information law', and he presupposes a wide knowledge of some of the most important contemporary writings on the issue. As such it is already informative to realise how wide the literature goes on this matter and by implication, of course, how well we should be read on this theme if we want to participate intelligently in the debates.

Midgley (1991), fully aware of the dramatic impact of developments related to the idea of an information society, wrote her very enlightening book *Wisdom, Information and Wonder* (note the interesting link between wisdom and information) and came forward with another view which one cannot help but take seriously. She is more constructive and less keen to sketch a revolutionary picture and to turn things upside down. We can certainly benefit from her constructive approach, and share her sense of wisdom to our advantage, especially regarding our theme, as will be indicated later on in the very next section when we discuss possible ways of dealing with this impact.

Mark Poster is one of the most productive and also prolific writers on the theme of the information society and the impact of information and electronic media on individuals and societies. The scope of the impact of electronic developments is fascinating as revealed in his following works: *The Mode of Information* (1990), *The Second Media Age* (1995), *What's the Matter with the Internet?* (2001) and *Information Please* (2006). As insightful as the reading of his analyses in these books are, just as impressive are the bibliographic details regarding the broader literature on these themes. Indeed a challenge for the information scientist and information worker to come to terms with these developments and the implications thereof for human beings and human societies. Poster (1990: 21) writes: '[t]hings are happening in the social fabric, things that are radically new and that are not well accounted for within the confines of the established positions.' Thorough attention needs to be given to and careful analyses need to be done about what is happening since 'dramatic changes in the reproduction, transmission, storage and retrieval of information profoundly affect the entire social system' (Poster, 1990: 71), and by implication individual human beings as well. This not only implies but demands radical new thinking about human beings, human subjectivity, language, society and societal relations and dynamics with a view to insightful information science and intelligent information work. The ordinary, standardised 'tools' or equipment of 'the established positions' are totally inadequate for this purpose. Nothing can more convincingly suggest the development and utilisation of new conceptual equipment than this argument.

Virilio's book came as a shock. The simple title tells it all, namely *The Information Bomb* (2000). Shocking as it may be, it calls for serious reflection about what we have to encounter in our domain of intellectual and scientific activities and endeavours. Virilio is certain that the avoidance of the catastrophic consequences of 'the information bomb' (like the destruction of societal relations or bonds (living alone together), the superficialisation of scientific practices, the creation of a monotheistic perspective on information and informational totalitarianism, etc.) urgently requires a radically different kind of thinking regarding 'the culture of informationalism' (Castells), in other words what is really needed is a newly invented set of conceptual equipment or capabilities.

A substantial part of the implications of the 'information bomb' are emphasised by Virilio in an interview with Friedrich Kittler (Virilio, 2001). Virilio is explicit about the harm that can be done by the information bomb. Pertinent issues mentioned by him are the following:

- People no longer meet face to face – disturbing.
- Information fundamentalism is a matter of real and great concern for its negative implications.
- There is not enough debate about the totalitarian dimensions of information.
- The excessive praise of interactivity may prove to be in some way a form of radioactivity.
- Although we are being told that the Internet is bringing us freedom we may also be wondering whether, through this illusion of information-induced freedom, a new uniformity is being implanted in a masked form.
- The disappearance of space made possible by the new technologies constitutes a profound loss.
- The loss of social bonds is linked to the demise of the proximate human being, the so-called living apart together (see Turkle's study on this theme, *Alone Together* (2011)).
- Information is being turned into a product of global enterprises and this tragedy is being sold to us as progress.
- The reduction of content which is happening here has destructive consequences.
- We are being confronted with a 'technological fundamentalism' in the sense of a 'monotheism of information' as the outcome of an intelligence without reflection on the past, and with it comes the greatest danger of all, the slide into the future without humanity, the ultimate aspect, perhaps, of the totalitarian dimension of information. (All the rhetoric about the post-human and the trans-human may prepare the way for this humanless future. It should perhaps be kept in mind – if at all possible – that humans are central, although machines are strongly and heavily pushed forward, but on the condition that humans are not central in a humanistic but in a humane sense.)

What are the ways to defeat this threatening challenge? We have to rethink – and thoroughly rethink – science and especially information science and the implications of this rethinking for information work. We have to force our way back towards usefulness, towards meaning, while realising that the total existence of humans is at stake. Dealing with this characterisation of the scope and depth of developments regarding information and the information society from so many angles and perspectives calls for new equipment, new ways of thinking in diverse respects. We should rethink our own involvement and kind of involvement with information and knowledge in view of these developments. In order to do so we have to become informed about information and its impact on society, on individuals, on knowledge, on ethics, on culture and politics, and on us. If it is true what these people (sociologists, architects, philosophers, historians, etc.) are saying, it poses a challenge to us to think about the implications of what they are saying. That is why I wrote an article about thinking (2010a) because this is our only and our very best piece of equipment! Let us start applying it.

### 4.3.2 What should be done about 'the information explosion'?

The information explosion is for our purposes here actually an umbrella term for the diversity of issues discussed in the above-mentioned publications that reflects the scope and impact of information and knowledge on individuals and societies.

It is important to note Cronin's characterisation of our field: 'Our primary interest in information is at the perceptual and conceptual level, in information as it is perceived by the senses, heard, read, seen, keyboarded and spoken *as opposed to* information engineering, defined in terms of the sub-atomic realm of bits, bytes and code' (Cronin, 1995: 60, my emphasis). To deal with this in any proper way possible what is desperately needed is 'the requisite variety to reflect the multi-dimensionality and inter-disciplinarity which the study of information demands at both the perceptual and conceptual level' (Cronin, 1995: 60). The 'information explosion' cannot be left unattended but we have to approach issues differently. There are indeed conflicting proposals and/or strategies. On the one hand, there is the techno-scientific approach that expects total salvation from technical means. On the other hand, there is the realisation that something much more humanly dramatic is required. In the first place the temptation must be resisted that salvation by technical means is and will be possible. Secondly, we should dig deep into the knowledge phenomenon, fathom its depths and multiplicities and tackle the problem from such an angle, an angle much closer and more true to reality than the reductionistic techno-scientific approaches we are bombarded with and forced to accept and comply with.

What is needed? How do we save ourselves? How do we deal with the 'information explosion' and its anxieties in a significant way? It may be wise to take heed of Midgley's suggestions but also of those of Michel Henry (2012) and Richard Wurman (1991). According to Midgley (1991) the following pertinent matters deserve attention:

- Human life absolutely needs *a conceptual framework*: it needs guiding myths; it needs morality (Midgley, 1991: 48; 72).
- Understanding, information, knowledge, wisdom should be knitted together as a unity (Midgley, 1991: 41, 43−45).
- What is not needed is the concealment or denial of dangerous facts or theories, but the supply of more and better facts, and even theories, to replace the dangerous ones.
- Imaginative work is needed ... We need to widen our imaginative experience (get some dreamwork done (reveries, fantasies) ... much needed exposure to colourful ideas and to the widest possible perspectives on reality as Foucault (1970: 169) mentions regarding Deleuze in this respect when he refers to 'the expanding domain of intangible objects that must be integrated into our thought'. Our refusal to do exactly that gives evidence of our severe intellectual and scientific poverty. An important contribution related to these insights is made by Michel Serres (1995). It may be very useful to study his book *Genesis* on his perspectives on 'multiple reality' and how to cope with and articulate it in a sensible way rather than merely ignoring it. His solutions are specifically relevant to information science's position as a science and can also help us to deal with the multi-faceted impact of the 'information explosion'.
- Relate academic specialities to one another, but especially to the rest of life and reality. This is when meaning is at issue − the movement must always be from part to whole (Midgley, 1991: 52−3) (see also Bohm, 2009) − more and better background thinking is required (Midgley, 1991: 48−9). The mere increase in information is futile. We already have too many facts. Again Bohm (2009) would add his voice to this and so would Dupuy before both of them. What is needed is to improve our ways of sorting them and relating them, connecting them ... meaningfully ... for human life in and under diverse

circumstances and for a diversity of situations and needs (Midgley, 1991: 53). 'It is a troublesome business, and it is not surprising that people have put up rather simple conceptual screens to protect them from seeing the need to do it' (Midgley, 1991: 53). It is important to note: 'protect them from seeing', that is force them into blindness.

> *Successful ideologies commonly make their impact by hammering at a single image, or small group of images, which expresses one side of the truth so vividly that they fill the reader's imagination, making it hard to remember that there is any other. Facts which will not fit it simply are not digested ... People dominated by such images are under a compulsion, which is felt as an actual obligation, to reduce everything else to these special terms.*
>
> *(Midgley, 1991: 48–9)*

Examples of this mentioned by Midgley are: Marxism's class war, behaviourism's conditioned rat, Freud's suppressed sexual desire, socio-biology's selfish gene.
- The art of thinking and world composition with a wider human life in mind should always be a matter of priority complementary to the orientation towards the solution of any specific need or problem (Midgley, 1991: 50).
- None of us can study anything properly unless we do it with our whole being (Midgley, 1991: 51): study what is, the whole of reality (*être*, being), with one's whole being, with who I am as a spiritual being (*nous*, spirituality, intellectuality) — know-how-to-do, plus know-how-to-live, plus know-how-to-think (theorise) will in a natural way emerge from this endeavour. To think is to be; to be is to think; not only *logos* but especially *nous* performs here. This should be a motto for information science, its method and information work. (See also Chapter 6 on the merits of this noetic endeavour.)

To summarise this different approach, set out in the points above, in the words of the physicist David Bohm:

> *What we need is not so much new scientific ideas, although these are still going to be of great interest. The question is how can science [including information science], when based on a fragmentary attitude to life [the attitude one finds in all scientific disciplines as they are currently pursued], ever understand the essence of real problems that depend on an indefinitely wide context? The answer does not lie in the accumulation of more and more knowledge. What is needed is* wisdom. *It is a lack of wisdom that is causing most of our serious problems rather than a lack of knowledge. [Note that these are the words of a renowned physicist and not a philosopher.]*
>
> *(Bohm & Peat, 1989: 13–14)*

When we want to explore wisdom in this context specific conceptual equipment is required. Wisdom is not a skill and requires thought of special quality. The mere fact that the information scientist is seen and described 'as a philosopher' (although long ago in the history of American librarianship by Shera) and thinks regularly of wisdom in terms of the ladder of data, information, knowledge, wisdom that information scientists are quite keen to quote without giving a thorough exposition of it, then it becomes more than a sensible option to explore. The identification of the librarian, the true librarian, as a sage (Melot, 2004) adds some flavour to the whole idea of the importance of wisdom as not something accidental or a silly misnomer. This emphasis is reinforced by Salanskis' discussion of the focus on 'the philosopher as a disseminator of meaningful knowledge on a wide scale', which can just as well be the focus for the information scientist and worker (Salanskis, 2007: 18–20).

And this exploration will, moreover, self-evidently lead to a post-scientific position. For the acknowledgement, the exploration, the embracement and cultivation of wisdom special and very specialised equipment is required. That wisdom, with the right equipment, will be seen and accepted as the most natural outcome speaks for itself.

### 4.3.3  Conceptual equipment or capabilities

What is in fact needed is very explicit conceptual equipment that will enable us to work in a new, totally different and more fruitful and inventive direction. The above discussions bring us close to a thorough rethinking of the conceptual equipment required for the newly articulated information science. The new equipment is strongly suggested in the following terms by a number of information scientists:

- the notion of an interscience and 'the force of the between' (Bougnoux, 1995);
- more recent supportive articulations in this regard by Stiegler (2012);
- the exploration of interconcepts and their cross-disciplinary value and significance (Wersig, 1992, 1993b);
- information power, especially how it can and should be related to the theory of plasticity (Frohmann, 1994; Malabou, 2008, 2010);
- conceptual outsourcing and access newly interpreted (Cronin, 1995).

In responding positively to these challenges as expressed in the notions suggested above 'information science might be enabled to become an exporter as well as an importer of ideas' (Warner, 2001: 252), but the condition would be to leave behind all allergies for new and different and even strange ideas and ways of thinking.

The belief is that the previous views lead up to this inevitable outcome: we need very special equipment. Denial of this can only lead to our embarrassment. The contribution of Michel Serres (2009) in a recent publication is significant. His emphasis on the future of the sciences in terms of the decisive interdisciplinary nature of all the sciences, and that reference should be made more to knowledge in its totality than to such and such particular knowledges, creates a very pertinent opening for a post-scientific position as promoted here. Information science is focusing on knowledge as such and can be considered to be an interdiscipline or even interscience rather than a mere discipline (Bougnoux, 1993; De Beer, 2005; Stiegler, 2012) and is as such the best possible qualifier for the notion of a post-science. We need to keep in mind though that a post-scientific position is not an unscientific position. Science is about knowledge and we are here engaged in the pursuit of knowledge in the full sense. Knowledge is never complete and for that reason inventions of new knowledges are constantly a possibility. New knowledges often emerge from combinations of existing knowledges. It will be necessary, however, to develop and exercise some important disciplined strategies in this regard so that this post-science does not loose its qualifier as a science proper. It therefore requires a fundamental rethinking and thorough reflection on what a science exactly means and what scientific knowledge really stands for. The traditionally accepted definition of science may be urgently revisited. But all knowledge need not be knowledge generated in exactly the manner the classical sciences have employed for some time now. This is not the only way to generate knowledge and perhaps not even the best way. As Serres (1997: 66) remarks: 'Only when we move outside disciplines invention – and that assumes always something new – will be a possibility.'

In addition to the post-scientific position which should be seen as the starting point of this new conceptual equipment, terminology Lyotard introduces to us, the idea of paralogical thinking and communication should in addition be embraced. This is also a favourite term of Lyotard but has been extensively discussed by Kent (1993) and deserves careful attention, especially in the context of information work related to knowledge development and dissemination and the importance of quality communication in this regard.

Our conversations and communications about our scientific endeavours and the solutions to individual and social problems, pursued along these lines, will differ substantially from the current situation. Wersig's idea of interconcepts introduces a new dynamic into the scientific pursuit and brings us immediately into contact with Bougnoux's notion of an 'interscience', a notion which has recently been reintroduced in a much wider context by Bernard Stiegler (2012). The idea of 'information power' introduced by Bernd Frohmann (1994) strongly emphasises the real impact of information, in the sense of the 'meaning to be achieved in total human existence', in individual and social situations. When this is combined with 'the theory of plasticity' of form-finding, form-giving and form-destruction, as developed by Catherine Malabou, we encounter a considerable complementation of our conceptual equipment. All these insights can give special dimensions to scientific communications. This can be further complemented by the ideas of Day (2008) in his effort to redefine information as well as knowledge within the context of a new notion of what information science might be if it wants to be a science for our times. Information is not merely bits and pieces but considerably more ... This comes close to what Wersig and Kuhlen would do when they want to rearticulate information as 'knowledge for action'. The idea of action emerging from our encounter with knowledge forms a key component of the conceptual equipment, together of course with the rearticulation of the human being in our context as an acting and communicating being (Wersig, 1993a, 1993b).

Part of the challenge posed to the consideration of conceptual equipment would be vocabulary building which reminds us of Cronin's idea of 'concept recruitment from cognate fields' (Cronin, 1995: 60). This should be a standard activity in the new inter-scientific context envisaged for information science without which it would not be possible to come to fruition. We should never forget how central the idea of language, words, terms and concepts are in all information-related activities. Language currently suffers from debasement and impoverishment and it needs to be rescued for the sake of the enrichment of any scientific position. Paralogical thinking can play part in this and so can interpretative thinking, both currently neglected.

We have to borrow from other fields, thinkers and scientists (Cronin's idea of 'concept recruitment') without draining or depleting the real and deeper meaning of the borrowed vocabulary. Therefore my suggestion would be as follows. We should take up a post-scientific position of science for information science in the sense of the postmodern condition of knowledge (Lyotard), as significantly explored by Wersig in the domain of our subject field, and in the sense of the multiple connective intellection, which is also acritical, according to the views of Michel Serres, as well as in the sense of a nomad activity (Deleuze & Guattari, 1987). It could make sense to include the notion of plasticity as developed by Malabou (the shaping, form-giving abilities of information). Bachelard's emphasis on the 'new scientific spirit' indicates that the idea of rethinking the sciences and developing alternative conceptual equipment are not at all far-fetched.

This idea of going beyond or outside the standard scientific approach (the subject/object divide and fixed methodologies) is also pushed further in a very significant way by others. Hayles (2005: 241−3), with her emphasis on 'a new kind of science' borrowed from Wolfram (2002) with a book by the same title, is a significant example. We have to focus on or develop or rely on 'narratives of a different kind' (Hayles, 2005: 243), and she discusses a few examples of this kind of narrative (the theoretical significance of certain films in this context) that offer a way out of the dichotomy. In this kind of narrative humans are not seen as subjects manipulating objects in this world. We need to keep in mind that the narratives against which she makes claims are narratives in which the subject/object dichotomy remains intact although they are already desperately searching for alternatives. Cinematic examples discussed by her include the Terminator and Matrix series and Blade Runner.

It is important to note the impact trans-disciplinarity has on the nature of knowledge. The multiple connective intellection coined by Michel Serres has already been suggested as an extremely relevant and meritorious, actually indispensable, focus in this regard. Implicit in this is, of course, the understanding of science quite differently from science in the traditional sense. Note the introduction by Salanskis, Rastier, and Scheps (1997). They emphasise that:

> *The study of texts is crucial for the sciences of the spirit or the human sciences. The emphasis on hermeneutics in the sciences of the spirit is generally speaking to be opposed to the canonical model of the natural sciences, although it remains true that more and more of the 'hard' sciences can no longer ignore hermeneutics or even have to admit that hermeneutics works even in them.*

This is despite Cronin's unfortunate scepticism about hermeneutics. They continue:

> *We are approaching for some time now a new epoch of interdisciplinarity, they emphasize. It is a fundamental aspect of the development of modern knowledges; there are profound reasons for research subjects to solicit the competence of several objectifying perspectives, several methodologies. Rather than being founded on the idea of the instrumentalisation of knowledges exploring the same referent,*

*interdisciplinarity starts to be conceived as the putting into an interpretative relationship of the languages belonging to the diverse branches of these knowledges ... At the same time that interpretation affirms itself as the preponderant modality of the dialogue between the disciplines interdisciplinarity imposes itself as a major object of study. Understanding humans as interpretative animals appears more and more as an essential task for the cognitive theorisation of intelligent behaviour and action ... Moreover, the question of interpretation is crucial for the epistemological understanding of the sciences, exact, natural or human, and finally for the contemporary rationality in its totality.*

*(Salanskis et al., 1997: 2−3)*

They continue further on the importance of information:

*It would be convenient to take the notion of interpretation as a guide in studying the sciences. Some questions are: To what extent is scientific rationality always of an interpretative nature? How do we understand the relationship between the interpretative discourse of the natural sciences and the sciences of the spirit? Perhaps the hierarchy of the sciences are in the process of losing its rigidity in view of the social sciences or sciences of the spirit becoming the real source of reflection and/ or interpretation, not so much through their methodology as through the hermeneutic gnoseology, proper to the cultural sciences [sciences of the spirit].*

*(Salanskis et al., 1997: 4, my translation)*

Complementary to this Stiegler (2012: 247−8) states explicitly: 'The structure of science appears to be essentially documentary; the document becomes, in other words, constitutive ... Documentarity is originary ...' If this is the case for science in general, all the more true is it for information science. Textuality is central and with it language, symbol and sign. It stands to reason that interpretation and the theory of interpretation, also called hermeneutics, becomes an important issue, without which neither information science nor information work can manage to move forward in any new direction.

## 4.4   The gap between information science and information work closes up

The anticipation of new knowledges and new practices, the immense task of both scientists and practitioners, for significant contributions to the renewal and the building of society, should flourish under the impact of this fresh, new and inventive exploration of an alternative scientific position for information science that does not of course and should never exclude the information worker. (See Chapter 8 for further discussion on the information and knowledge worker.)

What is it that is really needed? We might suggest:

- an awareness of knowledge's multiple manifestations, meanings, forms and interpretations;

- access to this knowledge purified from the 'dysfunctional attitudes and monothetic rhetoric' which have retarded growth for so long and the embracement of an inter-conceptual status for information science as well as concept recruitment from cognate fields;
- the extensive pursuit of connectivity which includes the inspired crossing of boundaries and the adventurous establishment of new connections that lead to inventions of a grand scope with inter-concepts as a central connecting drive;
- the expansion of vocabulary that accommodates these dramatic moves into the unknown;
- a sensitivity for 'information power' that can shape lives, knowledges, disciplines, subdisciplines and outcomes;
- the enhancement of compositional thinking as the single most important capacity to be built and never to be taken for granted, with a view to the future.

This is a tall order for theoreticians as for practitioners. But both are confronted with this desperate need for this new and vital equipment.

In the above examples we find a rich display of conceptual configurations that can be fruitfully pursued not only by information scientists but also by information workers. Conceptual enrichment is our main challenge and not difficult to pursue given the richness of language and vocabulary (scientific and otherwise). Nomad, multiple connective intellection (communication, transduction, interference, distribution, passages), interconcepts, postmodern conditions, information power, affinities, invention, irreduction, plasticity, narrative are all terms to be implemented in the new dispensation proposed for information science. Careful analyses of these terms and their role in the generation and dissemination of information/knowledge in society, of the environment (ecology) in which we operate and their applicability in this situation, of the spirit of our times and how it affects our needs and our activities and our solutions and strategies will be of the utmost significance. Such analyses, especially when pursued by means of transductive, compositional thinking, would be required for the meaningful invention of solutions that will guide, enlighten and shape both societies as well as individuals of all ranks in society. One thing we should agree on: wisdom is required.

The new conception of science with its implications for information practice would require a new methodological approach. As a matter of fact, a new methodology is a prerequisite for thinking in new and different ways about science. Rethinking science means rethinking method. Chapters 5 and 6 will address this and will contain the articulation of this new conception of method.

# References

Atlan, H. (1986). *Entre le cristal et la fumée*. Paris: Seuil.
Blair, D. (2006). *Wittgenstein, language and information: 'Back to the rough ground'*. Dordrecht: Springer.
Bohm, D. (2009). *On creativity*. London: Routledge Classics.
Bohm, D., & Peat, D. (1989). *Science, order and creativity*. London: Routledge.
Bougnoux, D. (1993). *Sciences de l'information et la communication*. Paris: Larousse.

Bougnoux, D. (1995). 'Qui a peur de l'information? In R. Capurro, K. Wiegerling, & A. Brellochs (Eds.), *Informationsethik*. Konstanz: Universitätsverlag.

Buckland, M. (2011). What kind of science can information science be? *Jounal of the American Society for Information Science and Technology, 63*(1), 1−7.

Cronin, B. (1995). Shibboleth and substance in North American library and information science education. *Libri*, 45: 45−63.

Day, R. E. (2004). Poststructuralism an information studies'. In B. Cronin (Ed.), *Annual review of information science and technology* (pp. 575−609). Medford, NJ: Information Today.

Day, R. E. (2008). *The modern invention of information: Discourse, history, and power.* Carbondale, IL: Southern Illinois University Press.

De Beer, C. S. (2005). Towards information science as an interscience. *South African Journal for Library and Information Science, 71*(2), 107−114.

De Beer, C. S. (2009). Let the new knowledge come: Atlas of knowledges. In *IX congress ISKO-Spain: New perspectives for the organization and dissemination of knowledge, acta del congreso* (Vol. 1, pp. 48−57). Universitat Politécnica de Valencia.

De Beer, C. S. (2010). The knowledge society: Refounding the socius. In M. D. Lytras (Ed.), *Best practices for the knowledge society: Learning, development, technology for all.* Berlin: Springer Verlag.

De Beer, C. S. (2011). Methodology and noology: Amazing prospects for library and information science. *South African Journal for Library and Information Science, 77*(1), 85−92.

Deleuze, G., & Guattari, F. (1987). *A thousand plateaus: Capitalism and schizophrenia.* Minneapolis, MN: Minnesota University Press.

Dupuy, J.-P. (2000). *The mechanization of the mind.* Princeton, NJ: Princeton University Press.

Fernandes, J. C., & Kobashi, N. Y. (2010). The complexity challenge: A contribution to the epistemological reflection regarding information science. In C. Gnoli, & F. Mazzocchi (Eds.), *Paradigms and conceptual systems in knowledge organizations.* Würzburg: Ergon Verlag.

Foucault, M. (1970). *Theatrum philosophicum. Language, counter-memory, practice.* Ithaca, NY: Cornell University Press.

Frohmann, B. (1994). Communication technologies and the politics of postmodern information science. *Canadian Journal for Information and Library Science, 19*(2), 1−22.

Gleick, J. (2012). *The information: A history, a theory, a flood.* London: Fourth Estate.

Hayles, K. N. (2005). *My mother was a computer: Digital subjects and literary texts.* Chicago: University of Chicago Press.

Henry, M. (2012). *Barbarism.* London: Continuum.

Kent, T. (1993). *A theory of communicative interaction.* Lewisburg, PA: Bucknell University Press.

Kuhlen, R. (2004). *Informationsethik: Umgang mit Wissen und Information in elektronischen Raumen.* Konstanz: UVK Verlagsgesellschaft.

Lash, S. (2002). *The critique of information.* Cambridge: Polity Press.

Latour, B. (1988). *The pasteurization of France.* Cambridge, MA: Harvard University Press.

Lecercle, J.-J. (1990). *The violence of language.* London: Routledge.

Malabou, C. (2008). *What should we do with our brain?* New York: Fordham University Press.

Malabou, C. (2010). *Plasticity at the dusk of writing: Dialectic, destruction, deconstruction.* New York: Columbia University Press.

Melot, M. (2004). *La Sagesse du Bibliothécaire*. Paris: L'œil neuf éditions.

Midgley, M. (1991). *Wisdom, information and wonder: What is knowledge for?* London: Routledge.

Morin, E. (1990). *Science avec conscience*. Paris: Seuil.

Poster, M. (1990). *The mode of information: Poststructuralism and social context*. Cambridge: Polity Press.

Poster, M. (1995). *The second media age*. Cambridge: Blackwell.

Poster, M. (2001). *What's the matter with the internet?* Minneapolis, MN: University of Minnesota Press.

Poster, M. (2006). *Information please: Culture and politics in the age of the digital machine*. Durham, NC: Duke University Press.

Salanskis, J.-M. (2007). *Territoire du sens*. Paris: Vrin.

Salanskis, J.-M., Rastier, F., & Scheps, R. (1997). *Hermeneutique: Textes, sciences*. Paris: PUF.

Serres, M. (1980). *Hermès V, passage du nord-ouest*. Paris: Minuit.

Serres, M. (1995). *Genesis*. Ann Arbor, MI: University of Michigan Press.

Serres, M. (1997). *The troubadour of knowledge*. Ann Arbor, MI: University of Michigan Press.

Serres, M. (2009). *Écrivains, savants et philosophes font le tour du monde*. Paris: Le Pommier.

Stiegler, B. (2012). *États de choc: Bêtise et savoir au XXIe siècle*. Paris: Mille et Une Nuits.

Stiegler, B. (2013). *Pharmacologie du front national, suivi du Vocabulaire d'Ars industrialis*. Paris: Flammarion.

SubStance (1993). Epistemocritique, 22 (2/3) (Special Issue).

Turkle, S. (2011). *Alone together*. New York: Basic Press.

Virilio, P. (2000). *The information bomb*. London: Verso.

Virilio, P. (2001). The information bomb: A conversation with Friedrich Kittler. In J. Armitage (Ed.), *Virilio live: Selected interviews*. London: Sage.

Warner, J. (2001). W(h)ither information science?/!. *Library Quarterly, 71*(2), 243−255.

Wersig, G. (1990). The changing role of knowledge in an information society. In D. J. Foskett (Ed.), *The information environment: A world view*. New York: Elsevier Science.

Wersig, G. (1992). Information science and theory: A weaver bird's perspective. In P. Vakkari, & B. Cronin (Eds.), *Conceptions of library and information science*. London: Taylor Graham.

Wersig, G. (1993a). *Fokus mensch*. Frankfurt am Main: Peter Lang.

Wersig, G. (1993b). Information science: The study of postmodern knowledge usage. *Information Processing and Management, 29*(2), 229−239.

Wersig, G. (1995). Information theory. In D. J. Feather, & P. Sturges (Eds.), *International encyclopedia of information and library science*. London: Routledge.

Wolfram, S. (2002). *A new kind of science*. New York: Wolfram Media.

Wurman, R. S. (1991). *Information anxiety: What to do when information doesn't tell you what you need to know*. London: Pan Books.

# Method/beyond-method: the demands, challenges and excitements of scholarly information work

**5**

## 5.1 Introduction: the essence and necessity of scholarly engagement

When we think of information science as an interscience (see Chapters 2–4), and when the philosophy of information is reflected upon in acritical terms (see Chapter 1), what emerges is a formidable and extremely exciting subject field filled with dynamic dimensions that invoke comprehensive promises of novel inventions that can take not only the subject field as such but also the workers in this subject field to new heights of insights and celebrations.

It requires sensible and thoughtful methodological renewals and commitments to come to terms, in a scholarly way, with the challenges and demands of a complex field in order to reach the promised excitements. 'A scholarly way' is the only way that can possibly comply with the challenges and demands pertaining to such an endeavour, since this intellectual disposition assumes the qualities required for these challenges, and that is the case despite the fact that scholarly work is nowadays in total discredit.

Why is it that scholarly work is so highly recommended, contrary to the views of many distinguished researchers and intellectuals (see Foster, 2005, on Bourdieu's critique of scholarly reason)? Its characteristics, as identified and described over a very long period of time by many thinkers, speak for themselves. A brief summary should suffice and will hopefully give some foretaste of what exciting possibilities it might offer (also see De Beer, 2003). A scholarly work is a work of thought. Gilles Deleuze writes: 'Everything depends on the value and sense of what we think. We always have the truths we deserve as a function of the sense of what we conceive, of the value of what we believe' (1983: 104). In other words, scholarly work goes beyond disciplinary boundaries, is not bound by them or limited to them. It draws lines to other disciplines, establishes connections and makes contributions to the field of knowledge as such, transcends demarcations and searches inexhaustibly for the ultimate in knowledge. The scholar always searches for more, is never satisfied with the minimum or with what is considered to be sufficient or not too difficult, or with what belongs to any particular subject field. For the true scholar the issues mentioned would represent the bare minimum.

Furthermore, it embraces what can be called a movement beyond method. It takes method and its usefulness for what it is, namely a made and constructed road, but accepts at the same time that the truly beautiful scenes cannot always and sometimes can never be seen from the road. It realises how much science has to do with chance and not only with necessity (Monod, 1979). It also reminds us of Gadamer's idea of 'the infinite of the unsaid' (1977), or of 'the unpredictable and unforeseen' of the mathematician Ekeland (1988), or of the crystal-like firmness and hardness on the one hand and the smokiness and vagueness of reality on the other according to the biologist Henri Atlan (1986).

In an answer to the question about what really makes a scholar, Gadamer writes:

> *That he has learned the methods. There is such a thing as methodological sterility, that is, the application of method to something not really worth knowing, to something that has not been made an object of investigation on the basis of a genuine question. It is imagination (Phantasie) that is the decisive function of the scholar. In this regard methods in science are paying dearly for their own progress − they sacrifice one of the most fruitful and creative human activities − imagination. (1977: 12)*

Added to this the following remarks by Bourdieu are significant:

> *The scholar is the person who knows how to apply theory in the true sense of the term, namely to look attentively on the outward appearance wherein what is present becomes visible and, through such sight − seeing − to linger with what shows itself. In such a way knowledge becomes possible and theory helps us to understand. The scholar is, in other words, also the visionary. Understanding calls for a special strategy which must be seen as a spiritual exercise aiming to obtain ... a true transformation of the view we take of others [of objects, things] in the ordinary circumstances of life. The welcoming disposition ... the capacity to take her [the thing or object] just as she is, in her distinctive necessity, is a sort of* intellectual love: *a gaze which consents to necessity in the manner of the 'intellectual love of God', that is to say, of the natural order, which Spinoza held to be the supreme form of knowledge. (1996: 24)*

One of the fundamental tasks of the scholar is reflection, that is thinking about the quality of my knowledge, the depth of my understanding, the clarity of my vision, and thinking about the obstacles in my way to knowledge constructed by my assumptions, prejudices and presuppositions, and my personal preferences and ideological blindfoldedness. The next section will certainly demonstrate why scholarly abilities are required and are highly necessary, especially when one wants to move into the realm of the beyond-method.

## 5.2 The complexity of the field of the research endeavours

Ample illustrations of the 'dizzy' and 'fussy' field of information and knowledge in its full complexity can be found in the themes researched by at least three renowned scholars in our field as reflected in some of their recent publications. The choice of scholars is a random one; there are many more. They are not the only ones working, with some immense impact, in our field. But all three of these scholars, one from Canada, one from the United States and one from Germany, are at least working at the heart of our subject field.

In other words, by using them to illustrate my point and to support my argument, I am trying to be truthful to what happens in information science and information work and I am for this very reason certainly not completely out of step. What their works especially call for is a unique and very enthused notion of thought that excites and takes us forward in so many respects, but this thought must be reflected in our methodological endeavours as well and not only in our appreciation of the richness and vastness of our field.

Their exploratory work and research endeavours have at least three major foci relevant to the perspective of this chapter, namely: the subject field of information science; adequate methodological considerations suitable for the field as it emerges through their endeavours; and the excitement of fresh and new findings as the result of their energetic scholarly work. Their insights, findings and proposals will enable us to reassess and reinvent parts of our subject field, or at least make us aware of the vastness and interdisciplinary nature of this field.

### 5.2.1   The research on the deflation of information by Bernd Frohmann (2004)

This study deals with information as a reified abstract object that must be revised for scientific information to be communicated in a significant but also useful way. Frohmann (2004: 8) states:

> *Under the spell of thought, representation, ideas, conceptual networks, proposi-tions, and conceptions of scientific work as primarily a highly abstract and theoret-ically oriented cognitive activity, and under the assumption that the pace of contemporary scientific work requires speeds of information transfer impossible to attain through the refereeing systems and print medium of the journal literature, information studies seeks other channels for the communication of scientific information.*

In order to achieve these alternative channels we should move away from 'the abstract idea of information' based on 'the conception of information as a particular kind of substance' implied by the above statement.

This work by Frohmann is not a solitary and isolated endeavour as the study clearly demonstrates, and it is also not the first of its kind, although not necessarily in the context of information science. In two consecutive publications (Gibbons et al., 1994; Nowotny, Scott, & Gibbons, 2001) the same problems have been addressed and similar critical comments have been made on scientific knowledge in general, including in a very specific way, of course, on the natural sciences. Specific attention has been given to 'the absence of, or the emptiness of its epistemological core' (Nowotny et al., 2001: 179–200). But even more than a decade earlier, Ian Hacking (1981) edited a fine booklet on 'scientific revolutions' – which can to a great extent be seen as a tribute to the well-known Thomas Kuhn – in which the idea of 'the pure knowledge of the sciences' is questioned.

What is encountered in Frohmann's study is a thorough and, according to many, a highly suspicious questioning of the accepted (very often in a highly uncritical way) notions in information science and works that are accepted as standard notions without which the activity of the science cannot proceed. Notions such as information, communication, knowledge, representation, transfer, theory, practice and many others are taken for granted and are accepted as the foundations of this science. In their substantialised form they contribute to an idealisation of science and scientific knowledge. In this context key roles are assigned to information seeking, information processing and the communication of information.

Frohmann finds the motivation for his critical strategy particularly in the sociology of science. It is well-known to what extent certain sociologists of science have studied extensively the work of scientists and especially science-in-progress in their explorations of how scientific facts are constructed. *Laboratory Life* by Latour and Woolgar (1986) is a prime example and one of the most influential in this regard, but there are certainly many more.

The heart of the matter is that questioning the core concepts or notions implies questioning the very landscape of information science as described by these notions. It means that the landscape is shifted or even turned upside down. The field looks differently and calls for a different way of dealing with it. Central activities in the field are at issue, namely information retrieval, information processing, the communication and transfer of information, the essential understanding of information itself, record studies and documentation, indexing and classification.

Although it is always difficult and risky to take things for granted, one fundamental implication of this questioning is that everything that has been taken for granted in the field needs to be rethought, and therefore also redefined and redescribed even in cases of defending, justifying and reconfirming the status quo. Moreover, the way in which the questioning is pursued implies that the demarcation of the field has been shifted and widened to a great extent. The challenges posed hereby to information scientists and information workers are multiplied. Although it was never a straightforward matter it is in view of these developments, if accepted, even less so.

It is by no means a matter of criticism for the sake of criticism. It is driven by the conviction that the scientific endeavours of a specific science are forced into dead-end streets because of the uncritical and consequently unwise acceptance of notions and strategies as fixed and final while overwhelming evidence to the contrary exists. The significant role of personal convictions, ideological inputs, prejudices and assumptions in establishing what science is and what constitutes a scientific fact are totally underplayed if not altogether ignored.

It is clear that research of this nature into the effectiveness and significance of scientific information transfer and communication requires investigations of a very subtle and complex nature which will be attended to in Section 5.3.

## 5.2.2   Research on language, philosophy and information
by David Blair (2006)

There could never have been any doubt about the central importance of language in the context of information science and the activities related to it. Although it is important, the attention given to language remains extremely limited, and even non-existent in most instances. It hardly formed a specific domain of investigation and exploration – another significant entity that has been taken for granted. All of us know exactly what language means, what it is, what it is used for and how it is used. The coming and increase in importance of semantics, semiotics and linguistics raised a few eyebrows but hardly more than that. The fashionable soon disappears. Even the efforts of Kuhlen (1986) with his enthusiastic study of information linguistics did not last very long and despite his significant insights and usefulness did not find ample support.

Blair proposes an answer to the question why issues of language and meaning are important to the study of information. When information is described we must mean something by these descriptions. Any study of information, dissemination of information or requests for information must be placed within the complex study of language and meaning (Blair, 2003). Any request for information must be put within the study of language and meaning. No information scientist and no knowledge and information worker can afford not to attend to the question of the central importance of language. Statements like these immediately and quite obviously show why philosophy should be involved as well. For this reason, Blair (2006: 2) poses the questions: Why language? – Why philosophy? – Why Wittgenstein?

Wittgenstein is of course one of the most influential, if not *the* most influential, philosophers of language of the twentieth century. In order to assess his value we have to acquaint ourselves with other philosophies of language as well. This is simply to emphasise why it is only the scholar who can cope with the demands.

According to Blair, anyone who accepts the importance of language in an information context should diligently attend to the significant views of Wittgenstein on language. We will highlight a few of the most significant of these insights as identified by him. He states that we have to be selective about what to take from the philosophy of language for our own work, because some are helpful and others not. In order to distinguish, however, we have to develop an understanding of the full scope of both language and our subject field (Blair, 2006: 4).

The first point to be made is that Blair takes 'the approach of the philosophy of language to be the fundamental examination of the issues of meaning'. It would be difficult to argue against the assumption that only meaningful information forms the heart of information science and work. In this regard the relationship between language and truth should not be disregarded since it is of vital importance although totally neglected.

There are clearly two different views on the meaning of language that have been developed and discussed extensively by linguists and philosophers over a long period: the logical formalistic approach or the abstract approach to language on the one hand, and the dynamics of ordinary language, also referred to as the material aspect of language, on the other. Depending on one's approach the outcomes and applicability will be determined. The first is a very obvious reductionist approach but it proved to be valuable and useful in many situations although it remains an impoverished view. The second approach is much more uncertain and contains risky elements because it refuses to accept any form of reductionism and prefers to give account of the full spectrum of the real.

This problem is well-illustrated by Wittgenstein's philosophy of language. One of the most central issues of concern for him is 'the determinacy of sense' which refers to the precision by which meaning can be defined. Gottlob Frege and Bertrand Russel believed that ordinary language (the material aspects of language) was not precise enough to represent the complexity and subtleties of meaning; we have to clarify in clear and unambiguous terms what we say about the world (in terms of the abstract aspects of language). The model for this approach would be the rigour of scientific method. What is needed then is a logical language that could faithfully model these complexities and subtleties of expression and that could be used to clarify whether statements of fact were true or false. This language could uncover the underlying logic of language so that language can be made more precise through the use of formal logic. Such logically perfect language is a language which 'has rules of syntax which prevent nonsense, and has single symbols which always have a definite and unique meaning' (see Blair, 2006: 4–5). This is of course a highly reductionist perspective on language, complying with the earlier mentioned abstract notion of language.

Initially Wittgenstein was sympathetic towards this view. As his thought matured he began to have serious misgivings about the ability of logic to model or represent the complex and subtle statements of language.

Not only was logic inadequate to this task, he thought, ordinary language itself was, if used properly, the best possible medium for linguistic expression, philosophical or otherwise. In short, Wittgenstein's thought evolved from a belief that problems of meaning in language could be clarified by logically analytic methods to a realisation that many of the unclarities of language were a result of removing statements from the context, practices and circumstances in which they were commonly used – what Wittgenstein called our 'forms of life'. What determined the truth or meaning of a statement was not some underlying logic, but how and in what circumstances the statement was used. Ambiguities in language are clarified not by logical analysis, but by looking at how the words or phrases in question are used in our daily activities and practices (Blair, 2006: 5).

The full scene of linguistic dimensions as sketched by Wittgenstein and developed by Blair for our scientific endeavours relate to notions such as language as city, language as labyrinth, language games and the founding of language in forms of life. Information must be differentiated in a similar way.

These two perspectives are decisive in deciding about 'the determinacy of sense', especially in so far as determinacy of sense is central not only to language but also to all information- related work. Wittgenstein's view of language is important for information-related activities, for example the study of information systems.

*Our current most widespread model of information systems is the computer model, in particular the 'data model' of information. This has been a very successful and robust model that has had a remarkably long history of implementation. Computers are, in a fundamental sense, logical machines, so that we might say that the current most popular model for information systems is the* logical model. *This logical model ... has worked well for providing access to the precise, highly determinate content of our data bases ... But as more and more of our information is being managed by computerized systems we find that we must provide access to less determinate information like 'intellectual content' of written text, images and audio-recordings ... These kinds of access are not as well served by the logical data model of information ... Current information systems are in some way victims of the success of the more determinate data model of information ... The data/logical model cannot always capture the subtleties of language necessary for the retrieval of precise intellectual content on large information systems ... As long as we believe that the precision of representation for data retrieval is possible* for all information systems, *we will run the risk of building ... dysfunctional systems − systems insensitive to the subtleties of language.*

*(Blair, 2006: 5, 6, 7)*

While pondering the significance of the above-mentioned insights it is important to realise how poor is the scientist/worker who has no understanding of these dynamic aspects of language. And again, let us not fool ourselves by claiming that we know what language means since such ignorance paves the way to stupidity, one of the sicknesses of our time, to sterility, and in the last analysis to fundamental boredom. At the same time, in a more positive sense, these considerations help us to assess the landscape of the information sciences not only in terms of its magnificent scope but also in terms of its significant positioning in the full spectrum of the sciences and scientific work − indeed a key position. The methodological challenges posed by these insights are formidable. How to cope and deal with the abstract dimensions of language is fairly straightforward. How to cope and deal with the material aspects of language is immensely problematic and difficult and cannot be allowed to escape the attention of information scientists and information workers. Instead of looking for an underlying logic of language as Russell suggested we need to look at how language is actually used, for it is not an underlying logic that clarifies what we mean, it's the context, activities and practices in which we use language that provide the fundamental clarification of meaning we are looking for.

The methodological implications for user studies, readership and writing stand to reason and will be explored further in Section 5.3.

### 5.2.3 The thorough and fundamental study of information ethics by Rainer Kuhlen (2004a)

This study does not afford us any room to relax. Kuhlen's research emphasises once more how complex and dynamic our field of study really is. Nothing is simple, and the simple is always the simplified. The way he links information ethics to philosophical ethics, to the ecology of knowledges and the link between knowledge ecology and information ethics, to freedom of communication, to questions of the digital divide and the encounter with knowledge and information in the electronic space, to problems of privacy and to the central question of to whom knowledge and information really belong (is this ownership a public or a private matter?), illustrates very significantly the nature of the complex and interdisciplinary dimensions of our subject field that calls for special investigative and thoughtful strategies and approaches.

The series of questions posed by him in the study shows in a pertinent way to what extent information ethics cannot and should never be seen as an isolated issue, isolated from ethics proper and isolated from the ecology of knowledge. The assumption is of course a thorough and comprehensive understanding of both by information scientists and information workers. By approaching the theme in this way Kuhlen (2004b) clearly identifies a number of issues that the information scientist and information worker should, in a general sense, attend to. Once this disposition becomes the standard practice information ethics becomes a very natural and significant part of the core of activities belonging to the field. Ethical issues are interweaved with information and knowledge issues (see also Kuhlen, 2010).

If it is true that information ethics cannot be understood without careful attention to ethics and to knowledge ecology, it is equally important that these fields of study, and especially the relevant themes emerging from both of these fields, require serious attention. Information ethics will simply not be intelligible without these contexts and may amount to nothing but insignificant and powerless sets of rules and codes that appeal to nobody. In order to respond intelligently to the demands of information ethics the pertinent questions posed by Kuhlen should be responded to by individuals in their personal capacities, attitudes and responsibility (Lecourt, 2011: 19). In view of the demanding and challenging nature of these issues Kuhlen suggests specific methodological foci that will be addressed in the next section.

## 5.3   Methodological demands and challenges and a situation beyond-method

The unconditional requirement for understanding, investigating and reflecting on such a diverse and complex field is, however, the adoption of a different than usual methodological approach since the standard and generally accepted approach is rather sterile, inadequate, unimaginative and even naive given the dynamic field in which it should be applied. The interscientific dimensions of this field of study are so rich and complex, and the acritical dimensions so manifold and dynamic, that no single method or number of methods in the ordinary sense will ever be adequate. The dynamics of this field lie beyond these methods and their strategies and competencies and beyond critique and criticism as it complies with these methods. It calls for a situation of beyond-method, of journeys off the beaten track.

### 5.3.1 The three researchers

Our three researchers have demonstrated in extremely able and competent ways how a situation beyond method is not only necessary but the only feasible approach in the light of their exploratory work. Each one links his own considerations of the field to appropriate and effective ways of dealing with the happenings in this field as articulated by each of them.

### Bernd Frohmann

When we have to deal with deflated information and its alternatives the scope for exploration expands immensely. The traditional methodological approaches are inadequate and simply not suitable to respond to this situation. (See Frohmann (1994) for an exploration of discourse analysis as an alternative methodological approach.) In a later publication he again touches on the problem of method when he writes:

> *Discourse analysis presents information studies with an opportunity to revisit and refresh its historical interest in documents. It also connects with documentalism's historical insistence on the social spaces that documents help constitute and maintain. The method's focus on the institutional practices governing the production, organization, circulation and availability of documents engages with a far wider range of social practices than is usually considered by the field's emphasis – an equally traditional emphasis – on the performance and efficiency of information systems. It also provides a neglected social context for studies concerned primarily with the satisfaction of individual information needs. The resources it makes available – the conditions of the existence of statements, the practices with them and their stability – widens the field's pedagogical and research opportunities.*
>
> *(Frohmann, 2001: 14)*

In his book, Frohmann pleads for a multiple approach and practises it as well. One of his aims with strong methodological implications is to show 'how rich and varied the practices with scientific documents can be, especially compared to the simplistic idea that there is no more to the informativeness of a document than what happens in the mind of someone who understands it' (Frohmann, 2004: 16).

### David Blair

In our dealings with language as a major characteristic of the subject field, Blair is explicit about suitable methodological strategies equipped for the challenges posed by the presence of language and meaning at the heart of our subject field.

What is called for is an explicit anti-reductionistic approach, or in the words of Latour 'a strategy of irreduction, the disciplined and determined refusal to reduce at all cost' (1988: 212; see Chapters 2 and 4 in the present volume).

A core methodological invention may be linked up with this strategy against reductionism when Blair writes:

> If the indefiniteness of words or expressions is resolved by a consideration of their context or circumstances of occurrence, then it is no great intellectual leap to see that the indefiniteness of the language of representation and searching used by information systems might be resolved in a similar manner. This means that information systems are not context free but are situated in an important and essential way. They are influenced by the context and circumstances of their use, in particular they must be considered part of the common activities and practices in which they are used, and an understanding of these activities and practices may be necessary for the full potential of an information system to be exploited.
>
> (Blair, 2006: 23–4; see also Part III of his book for a detailed discussion of this point)

Consider also Blair's remarks on language, thinking, the articulation of needs and the determination of the usefulness of the information where it is stated that we live in language the same way we live in our cities (Blair, 2006: 12–13). Language offers us many alternative ways to say the same thing (see Blair, 2006: 14–15). It reminds one of the familiar statement by Martin Heidegger that language is 'the house of being'.

## Rainer Kuhlen

The ecology of knowledge that features as the basis for information ethics poses its own methodological challenges that can in no way be accommodated by traditional textbook recipes for methods. The dynamics is of such a nature that thought of a very special nature becomes a major substance for the method to be applied, especially to bring about the transition from an ecology of knowledge to an information ethics. With regard to ethical subjectivism and cultural relativism Kuhlen devotes a substantial paragraph in his book to the methodical handling of matters of information ethics: the descriptive, normative, meta-theoretical, discourse-theoretical handling is addressed (Kuhlen, 2004a: 37–42). From his reflection on ethical theories it becomes clear that the questions posed by information ethics are the fundamental questions of ethics as such: How do we want to live? How do we want our children and their children to live? In what does humanness consist? In what consists a just, a sustainable societal organisation? What are good, correct, perhaps even fair relationships? These are questions information scientists are called upon to respond to.

### 5.3.2   On the way to a position beyond-method

It is clear that the methodological moves made by our examples take us far beyond the traditional method route and put us strongly on the route of a position beyond-method. Despite their radical redescription of our methodological alternatives it still seems as if it is not radical enough in the sense that they manage to really take us beyond method, but even more: that they do not manage to take us far enough into the domain of real excitement and invention. For that we need much more, although this more is not at all unrelated to their insights and contributions. Traces in this direction are clearly identifiable but not adequately explored.

Some remarkable studies on this theme of methodological alternatives have been published. Here only three examples will be emphasised.

## Edgar Morin

His guidance in this respect of a beyond-method, as worked out in the series of publications with the title *La Méthode* (six volumes), is crucial. He firmly states:

> *We are in need of a method of knowledge that translates the complexity of the real, recognises the existence of beings and approaches the mystery of things ... The method of complexity demands the conceptualisation of the relationship between order/disorder/organisation; the refusal to reduce phenomena to their constitutive elements or to isolate them from their environments; the rejection of the dissociation of the problem of the knowledge of nature from the nature of knowledge.*
>
> *(Morin, 1977: 3–4, my translation)*

This, he says, is 'the voyage to the search for a mode of thought that would respect the multidimensionality, the richness, the mystery of the real and that would know that the cerebral, cultural, social and historical determinations that subject all thought co-determine the objects of knowledge. This is what I call complex thinking' (Morin, 1980: 10, my translation).

According to him it is self-evident that a rejection of these 'a-methodical' approaches would lead to 'a pathology of knowledge that materialises in the increase of ignorance and in the mutilation of knowledge' (Morin, 1986: 13–14, my translation). Equally crucial is his work on paradigm, especially his focus on 'the science of the knowing mind, or noology' that is capable of dealing with the paradigmatic knot as the space or place where 'the multi-determined character of knowledge finds expression which has its determinations in the individual, anthropological, noological, socio-cultural and psychoanalytical structures of the knowing mind' (Morin, 1983: 11–12).

## Michel Serres

Of similar importance is the work of Michel Serres. These thinkers are both adamant about the shortcomings of the traditional methodological approaches. Serres writes: 'We have at our disposal tools, notions, and efficacy, in great number; we lack on the other hand, an intellectual sphere free of all relations of dominance. Many truths, very little goodness. A thousand certainties, rare moments of invention' (Serres & Latour, 1995: 136). Compare in this regard also his remarks on method when he states that repeating a method is profoundly boring and nothing but a kind of laziness (Serres & Latour, 1995: 100), hence their keenness to propose other more thoughtful and inventive methodological avenues to be explored for responsible research.

## Paul Feyerabend

Their approaches are not far removed from the ideas of Feyerabend, perhaps a bit more known to some of you, as these ideas are proposed and worked out in his highly acclaimed book *Against Method* (1977). Here we are confronted with a really anarchistic perspective on methodological issues. Paraphrasing two remarks by him would clearly suggest the direction to be taken. He is emphatic about the fact that the insistence on the rules of method would certainly not have improved matters, but would much rather have arrested progress (Feyerabend, 1985: 13). And he also emphasises that case studies have shown that a blunt application of 'rational procedures' would not have given us a better science or a better world, but nothing at all (Feyerabend, 1985: 16).

Why is it necessary to push for the ultimate?

## 5.4   The rewards and excitements of scholarly work

The true nature of scholarly work makes it impossible to settle for less. Its eagerness and enthusiasm leaves nothing untouched. As Bohm and Peat (1989: 14) emphasised in view of the question *how can science ever understand the essence of real problems*?: 'The answer does not lie in the accumulation of more and more knowledge. What is needed is *wisdom*. It is a lack of wisdom that is causing most of our serious problems rather than a lack of knowledge.' The researcher/inventor needs to move into the sphere of the beyond-method where an acritical approach leaves criticism behind as a sterile ideological strategy and pursues knowledges and insights that bring about breakthroughs regarding static situations. This is of course a more demanding and challenging venture than 'mere research' and its stereotypes. This sphere represents the risky field of uncertainty and the mystery of never-ending explorations but also of adventures. This sphere calls for thought pursued in a totally different dimension than the type of thinking that normally would accompany most of the methodical inputs in scientific and research work. Edgar Morin (1991) in his study on *Ideas* refers to the noological domain and the noosphere in order to articulate this type of thinking. He also introduces the important notion of complex thinking called for by complex situations.

At the same time this thinking manages to comply with the true nature of the subject related to the information and knowledge field, as suggested above, that offers itself as the domain where 'light' is ignited that exorcises the darkness of ignorance, but also where 'formative activities' are taking place that allay chaos and disorder. This becomes the truly exciting part of the involvement with committed research and inventions in the field of information science and information work. It contributes to the explorations and the disclosures of possible significant futures for societies and individuals that are inclined to very often gyrate and meander in a world of the total or relative absence of meaning.

Nothing in the line of excitement can really be compared with the experience of 'I see' and 'I find'! These experiences are unique and cannot be fully described in words.

Against this background a truly scholarly approach with its special focus and qualities can comply with the demands and challenges of this complex field posed to novel methodological endeavours and can offer the so much hoped for excitements related to the invention of new futures related to knowledge and information exploration. Scholarly work in the true sense of the word, in its pursuit of creativity, is in full compliance with this suggested methodological approach. 'Creation resists death by reinventing life' (Serres, 1997: 100). This has to do with the proper functioning of intelligence in institutions, in the search for a thorough understanding of the theoretical as well as the practical dimensions of the information and knowledge sphere, 'out of regard for the health of life and mind' (Serres, 1997: 136).

# References

Atlan, H. (1986). *Entre le cristal et la fumée: Essai sur l'organisation du vivant.* Paris: Seuil.

Blair, D. (2003). Information retrieval and the philosophy of language. *Annual Review of Information Science and Technology, 37,* 3–50.

Blair, D. (2006). *Wittgenstein, language and information: 'Back to the Rough Ground.* Dordrecht: Springer.

Bohm, D., & Peat, F. D. (1989). *Science, order and creativity.* London: Routledge.

Bourdieu, P. (1996). Understanding. *Theory, Culture and Society, 13*(2), 17–37.

De Beer, C. S. (2003). Scholarly work: Challenges, excitements and promises. *Mousaion, 21* (1), 117–136.

Deleuze, G. (1983). *Nietzsche and philosophy.* London: Athlone Press.

Ekeland, I. (1988). *Mathematics and the unexpected.* Chicago: Chicago University Press.

Feyerabend, P. (1977). *Against method.* London: New Left Books.

Feyerabend, P. (1985). *Science in a free society.* London: Verso.

Foster, R. (2005). Pierre Bourdieu's critique of scholarly reason. *Philosophy and Social Criticism, 31*(1), 89–107.

Frohmann, B. (1994). Discourse analysis as a research method in library and information science. *Library and Information Science Research, 16*(2), 119–138.

Frohmann, B. (2001). Discourse and documentation: Some implications for pedagogy and research. *Journal of Education for Library and Information Science, 42*(1), 12–26.

Frohmann, B. (2004). *Deflating information: From science studies to documentation.* Toronto: Toronto University Press.

Gadamer, H.-G. (1977). *Philosophical hermeneutics.* Berkeley and Los Angeles, CA: University of California Press.

Gibbons, M., Limoges, C., Nowotny, H., Schwartzman, S., Scott, P., & Trow, M. (1994). *The new production of knowledge: The dynamics of science and research in contemporary societies.* London: Sage.

Hacking, I. (Ed.), (1981). *Scientific revolutions.* Oxford: Oxford University Press.

Kuhlen, R. (1986). *Informationslinguistik.* Tübingen: Max Niemeyer Verlag.

Kuhlen, R. (2004a). *Informationsethik: Umgang mit Wissen und Information in elektronischen Raumen.* Konstanz: UVK Verlagsgesellschaft.

Kuhlen, R. (2004b). Informationsethik. In R. Kuhlen, T. Seeger, & D. Strauch (Eds.), *Grundlagen von Information und Dokumentation*. Munich: K.G. Sauer Verlag.

Kuhlen, R. (2010). Ethical foundations of knowledge as commons. In *Proceedings of the international conference commemorating the 40th anniversary of the Korean society for library and information science*, Seoul, 8 October. Online at: <http://creativecommons. org/licen/by-sa/3.0/>.

Latour, B., & Woolgar, S. (1986). *Laboratory life: The construction of scientific facts*. Princeton, NJ: Princeton University Press.

Lecourt, D. (2011). *Contre la peur: De la science à l'éthique, une aventure infinie*. Paris: PUF.

Monod, J. (1979). *Chance and necessity*. London: Collins Fount Paperbacks.

Morin, E. (1977). *La méthode: 1. La nature de la nature*. Paris: Seuil.

Morin, E. (1980). *La méthode: 2. La vie de la vie*. Paris: Seuil.

Morin, E. (1983). Social paradigms of scientific knowledge. *SubStance, 39*, 3−20.

Morin, E. (1986). *La méthode: 3 La connaissance de la connaissance*. Paris: Seuil.

Morin, E. (1991). *La méthode: 4. Les Idées: Leur habitat, leur vie, leurs moeurs, leur organisation*. Paris: Seuil.

Nowotny, H., Scott, P., & Gibbons, M. (2001). *Rethinking science: Knowledge and the public in an age of uncertainty*. Cambridge: Polity Press.

Serres, M. (1997). *The troubadour of knowledge*. Ann Arbor, MI: University of Michigan Press.

Serres, M., & Latour, B. (1995). *Conversations on science, culture and time*. Ann Arbor, MI: University of Michigan Press.

# Methodology and noology: Amazing prospects for library and information science **6**

## 6.1 Introduction

In the previous chapter I discussed the notion of beyond-method, indicating that method in the ordinary sense of the word is totally inadequate for information science research due to the complexity and the comprehensive scope of the issues that we encounter in our subject field, and especially if we think of information science as an interscience. This statement was explored and justified in terms of the exemplary and formidable work done by three information scientists, namely David Blair (2003, 2006) on language, Bernd Frohmann (1994, 2001, 2004) on the deflation of information and Rainer Kuhlen (1986, 2004a, b) on information ethics and knowledge ecology. I ended my chapter in a very sketchy way with a few closing remarks on the relevance of the equally important work for us working in information science and in information services conducted by two internationally renowned intellectuals, Edgar Morin and Michel Serres, a sociologist and a philosopher of science, respectively. Their relevance for us relates to the fact that they both accept the challenge of the complexity of reality, of the world in which we live, and all related issues. They work out ways to deal and cope with the dynamics of these issues in the most significant way possible. They both have special ways of including information as central to their work, despite their different disciplinary backgrounds and engagements. This fact gave me the freedom to expect from their work, given their enthusiasm about the central place of information in society and life, the provision of significant insights into our own situation. Immediately after this was realised I started exploring these bodies of work for their possible benefit to us. This chapter is my effort to articulate in short their valuable contributions on behalf of our scientific and service activities.

This approach was justified and reinforced by the invitation to a library and information science and services research symposium with the formidable characterisation of our age and its societal dynamics in the following words: 'The modern information society is a dynamic and restless system.' If this is an accurate description — and I am convinced that it is — then we need to be extremely resourceful in our ways of dealing with such a reality. The following terms feature in a significant way: dynamic, restless, system, society and information. All these terms and related new ways require special focus and attention and not the kind of attention that we are used to and that is normally given.

Information Science as an Interscience.

The problem we encounter here is the following. Our standard, accepted methods cannot really help us here. These methods are still based on 'a flat world assumption' as is our policies, strategies and skills — all of which are based on a deterministic, linear approach and a cause-effect strategy. As such it cannot give account of the words dynamic, restless and complex. This system is simply too movable and fluctuating. There are too many dimensions. We need more, even more than reason alone. We have to move beyond method, beyond mere rationality, in order to cope and get real access and develop understanding. We have to move into another dimension, onto a totally new level of reality and into a different dimension or mode of thought — into another domain, the domain of ideas rather than problems. We have to start thinking differently. It seems as if we have to deal with two worlds.

Because science is a dynamic activity it constantly reviews itself, asks questions about itself and always looks for something new from many perspectives and from many people. Examples of such a critical and concerned questioning approach are Bachelard (1934), Bohm and Peat (1989), Bourdieu (1991, 1996, 2001), Dupuy (1990), Feyerabend (1977, 1985), Gibbons et al. (1994), Hacking (1981), Husserl (1970), Latour and Woolgar (1986), Nowotny, Scott, and Gibbons (2004), Stengers (1997, 2000, 2006, 2013), Stengers and Schlanger (1991) and many others. Chapters 2 to 4 attended to this quite extensively. The methodological implications of such a new scientific approach is now at issue. These questions, critiques and possible alternatives are in a very distinguished and convincing way explored by two scholars of a high international standing, namely Edgar Morin and Michel Serres, already mentioned in the previous chapter.

What I am trying to sketch and what is referred to here, in line with Edgar Morin's suggestions, is noology, or 'the science of the knowing mind', with its focus on the fullness and complexity of reality. The mode of thought that can effectively cope with this vast and complex challenge is what Michel Serres calls our 'multiple, connective intellection' which can penetrate all the respective areas and establish links between them. If we are serious about these challenges and want to explore this 'restless dynamic system' in its full complexity and contribute sensible responses to those challenges, we can hardly do better than look in more detail at the work done by Morin and Serres.

Under the general theme 'La Mèthode' ('The Method') Morin published six books with the following foci: nature, life, knowledge, ideas, humans and ethics. As is evident, these foci cover reality in its fullness. It can also be referred to as covering *phusis* (physical reality), *bios* (living reality) and *anthropos* (human reality). These themes demarcate the comprehensive dimensions of this system, this society, this world, and the knowledge we need to cope with all of this. The restless dynamic system is not only restless, but also very complex. We must be careful not to confuse the direct and immediate context with the wider context which mostly happens when we encounter problems. A problem never, or hardly ever, appears in isolation; it always appears in a context and always in an even wider context as well. The immediate context is important; the wider context explored in his six volumes on 'The Method' is even more important. It constitutes the ecology of our knowledge of the world. How to cope with these problematic settings requires special qualities. Morin adds two books to these six that are very helpful as significant introductions to the six volumes: *Introduction à la pensée complexe* (*Introduction to Complex Thinking*, 1990a) and *Science avec conscience* (*Science with Conscience*, 1990b). Their titles speak for themselves. For the full picture these two should be read together with the six. He suggested a special kind of thinking, namely complex thinking! This opens the door for Michel Serres.

Under the general theme 'Hermès', Michel Serres published five books with the following themes: communication, interference, transduction, distribution and the north-west passage. All five of them are very pertinent to our work as knowledge workers. Communication speaks for itself; interference can also be seen (according to Serres himself) as inter-reference; transduction is precisely what we have to do from day to day – translating information from one source to one or other destinations; distribution is what should have happened to information as reworked knowledge in order to get it to its appropriate needful, problem-ridden context and situation; passages are made between disciplines, sometimes almost undoable, in order to find the appropriate bit of applicable knowledge from wherever it may be required: *from myth to philosophy, to science, to literature*. He formulates the core of his message as follows and this formulation is most applicable to the knowledge worker, especially when facing huge academic libraries with millions of books which force upon us such a massive overwhelming encounter. He says that what we encounter is massive, overwhelming, but 'we must nevertheless try to see on a large scale; [to think big], to enjoy a multiple, and at times a connective intellection' (Serres, 1980: 24).

What both Morin and Serres are exploring and emphasising is the almost desperate call for a special kind of thinking, especially in times when we are inclined to neglect and underestimate the true importance of human thinking and the human mind.

## 6.2 The methodology of complexity of Edgar Morin: A noological situation beyond-method

What exactly is this noology? It is a play with ideas, a play of ideas; it is a matter of linking and connecting ideas and of allowing ideas to emerge, to appear, to become active. According to Morin, it is a move into the sphere of ideas – the noosphere. What needs to be mentioned is that this noosphere is not an abstract, totally inaccessible domain. No, it is close by; it is here, precisely here where we, all of us – LIS (Science) and LIS (Services) – are working and thinking. It links and connects science and services in order to become a forceful energy in the transformation and informatisation of society! Without this strong connection both science and service come to nothing. We cannot avoid it; we cannot escape from it. I will explore it under the methodology of complexity of Morin who describes a noological situation beyond-method. Noology is the human thought capacity to come to terms with the two essential dimensions of the knowable, namely the measurable and the immeasurable (or even the measureless) (Bernardis & Hagene, 1995). These two dimensions (or two worlds), and the necessity to keep them linked in an intricate way are well articulated by a number of scientists from a diversity of so-called scientific disciplines: Atlan (1986), Ekeland (1988), Monod (1979), Weizenbaum (1984), Wersig (1990) and Serres (1995). Many more can be added to this list.

The *Introduction to Complex Thinking*, and Fortin's (2008) elaboration of Morin's methodology offer an excellent orientation for 'The Method'. Together, the six books cover the vast field of knowledge, from the physical to the biological to the human and the ethical. Books 5 and 6 orchestrate all the themes of the preceding books in a new synthesis, realising the synthesis of a life of reflection on humans and on the contemporary world. They constitute the achievement of the *oeuvre* of Morin that consists of confronting the challenge and the difficulty of thinking the complexity of the real in order to come to an understanding of this real. The information and the knowledge that is the concern of information science in its efforts to understand is knowledge of and information about this real in its fullness.

Edgar Morin's guidance in this respect of a beyond-method, as worked out in the six volumes, is crucial. Note his main themes as made explicit in the subtitles: science of science, knowledge of knowledge, the life of life, ethics, ideas (their habitat, morals, life and organisation) and the humanity of humanity (about human identity). All these exciting themes are interconnected in various ways and are organised around the central notion of method, and that makes them even more exciting and inspiring. He stated firmly:

> *We are in need of a method of knowledge that translates the complexity of the real, recognises the existence of beings, and approaches the mystery of things ... The method of complexity demands the conceptualisation of the relationship between order/disorder/organisation, the refusal to reduce phenomena to their constitutive elements, or to isolate them from their environments, and the rejection of the dissociation of the problem of the knowledge of nature from the nature of knowledge.*
> *(Morin, 1977: 3—4, my translation)*

This, he says, is 'the voyage to the search for a mode of thought that would respect the multi-dimensionality, the richness, the mystery of the real, and that would know that the cerebral, cultural, social and historical determinations that subject all thought co-determine the objects of knowledge. This is what I call complex thinking' (Morin, 1980: 10, my translation). It is according to him self-evident that a rejection of these 'a-methodical' approaches would lead to 'a pathology of knowledge' that materialises in the increase of ignorance and in the mutilation of knowledge' (Morin, 1986: 13—14, my translation). Equally crucial is his work on paradigm (already explicitly emphasised in the previous chapter), especially his focus on 'the science of the knowing mind, or noology', that is capable of dealing with what he calls the 'paradigmatic knot' as the space or place where 'the multidetermined character of knowledge finds expression which has its determinations in the individual, anthropological, noological, sociocultural and psychoanalytical structures of the knowing mind' (Morin, 1983: 11—12).

The six volumes form a whole, a complete work that covers the vast field of knowledge, from the physical and biological to the ethical. Volumes 5 and 6 orchestrate all the themes of the preceding volumes in a new synthesis, realising the synthesis of a life of reflection on the human being and on the contemporary world. It constitutes the point of arrival of the great work of Morin which consists in confronting the challenge and the difficulty to think the complexity of the real. This magnificent *oeuvre* is typified at the start of the twenty-first century as 'a new reform of understanding' analogous to the undertakings by Spinoza, Leibniz or Descartes three centuries ago (see Fortin, 2008: 61). 'Reform' always appears in a period of crisis which must clarify the steps of humanity on its way, still powerless though, to accomplish itself as humanity.

This new reform also represents a new vision. It opens up new epistemological perspectives. Two worlds, or rather two visions of the world, confront each other: The one inherited from modernity and a classical vision of science; the other, a rupture from modernity and inseparable from new developments in science (thermodynamics, microphysics, astrophysics) (Morin, 1977: 95). Here follows a brief summary of Fortin's overview (2008). The first is founded on the ideas of order, determinism, necessity, clarity, certainty and measurement; the second is founded on the unity of order and disorder, on the impossibility of eliminating uncertainty, ambiguity, chance and risk — two related and interdependent visions of the world, united by a common trunk (the progress of science and the progress of thought) but incapable of letting dialogue and communication emerge between them. 'The Method' is not an indictment against science but is an effort on behalf of science, an open, non-reductive, reflexive and self-critical — even acritical — science. It is a road, a voyage, that is the search for a way of thinking capable of confronting the complexity of the real, able to recognise the wealth and the mystery of the real and to respect the multi-dimensionality of physical, biological, social, cultural and cerebral determinations that all knowledge and all thought undergo. Of this we find ample demonstration in library material and collections. Every volume can be read separately, but each of them contains constitutive dimensions of the total (Fortin, 2008: 54).

It is therefore really necessary to read the volumes on 'The Method' as a totality, as a multi-step in a chain that, from articulation to articulation, searches to encourage and effectuate communication between the great spheres of knowledge: *phusis*, *bios* and *anthropos*. Each volume is buckled to the following which buckles itself to the previous, constituting the unity of a work, the unity of thought, which makes itself going forward, and which nourishes itself. The *knowledge of knowledge* is at the heart of all these buckles. One can effectively read 'The Method' by reading the six volumes in couples:

- *Volumes 1 and 2* — the idea of complexity (and thus of organisation) applied to the physical, living and social organisation. The first buckle is the physic-bio-anthropo-sociological and the recognition of the complexity at the quadruple niveau of the physical, biological, human and social (See Morin, 1977 & 1980).
- *Volumes 3 and 4* — the idea of complexity (and thus of organisation) applied to knowledge and to ideas. The epistemological buckle returning in feedback to the preceding buckle; the recognition of the complexity of knowledge and of the complexity of ideas (noological niveau) (See Morin, 1986 & 1991).

- *Volume 5 and 6* — the idea of complexity (and thus of organisation) applied to the human being, to society and to ethics. Anthropo-socio-politico-ethical buckle returning in feedback to the preceding buckles. Recognition of complexity at the quadruple niveau of the human, the social, the political and the ethical (See Morin, 2001 & 2004).

If we search for a method in the sense of a totality of rules or a programme commanding action (like the *Discourse on Method* of Descartes), and as a support for our own quasi-methods, we will not find it. What we are going to find in 'The Method' is a totality of ideas or principles (these principles of complexity) that Morin applies to different objects covering the vast field of knowledge, from the physical and the cosmological to the ethical. The whole of 'The Method' (the whole work) rests in the first place on the sentiment of complexity of which the positive basis is the universal recognition of complexity. *Phusis* is complex. Society is complex. Thought (and knowledge) is complex. Politics is complex. Ethics is complex. Everything is complex.

'The Method' is a kind of a spiral movement which crosses and explores different territories in crossing and exploring different knowledges in order to make communicate that which does not communicate but must communicate: *phusis*, *bios* and *anthropos*. They are, all of them, connected. This calls for a reorganisation in the chain of knowledge, which calls for a constant combat and a struggle against all modes of disjunctive, reductive and simplifying thought. The first enemy of complexity is simplification: reductive, idealist, atomising, totalising, systemic and cybernetic. It is this enemy that Morin, through the whole of 'The Method', tries to track down in assuring the betting for the 'transformation of his conviction about complexity into a method of complexity' (Morin, 1980: 457). And this method, if it can formulate itself, can only formulate itself at the end, because method is road, a road not traced in advance, as we do as a matter of habit, but a road which makes itself or is made in the process of marching or walking (Fortin, 2008: 88−9).

The two additional books, already mentioned, can help one to unlock the dense and comprehensive six volumes of 'The Method', namely *Introduction à la pensée complexe* (1990a) and *Science avec conscience* (1990b). It is all in all either a matter of understanding that can take us forward, or rather a fatal lack of understanding. The *Introduction* is a small book constituting a regrouping of a number of texts, and offers six well-structured chapters that serve as an introduction to the problem of complexity: 'If the complex is not the key to the world, but the challenge to be confronted, complex thinking is not that which avoids or suppresses the challenge, but that which helps to relieve it and by times even enables one to overcome it' (Morin, 1990a: 11, my translation). As a pedagogical text of information well put together, *Introduction à la pensée complexe* can be a way to penetrate 'The Method' without entering straightaway through the main gate, but entering nevertheless, familiarising oneself with the notions and problematic of complexity. This is not only the challenge Morin faces, but is the challenge posed to each and everyone of us (see Chapters 4 and 5 in Morin, 1990a). Effectively it is a small text that will age well — the more one reads it, the more it grows.

## 6.3 The acritical anti-method of Michel Serres: Multiple connective intellection

In order to deal with the complexity of the real in an exhaustive way we need to complement and amplify the work of Edgar Morin on noology with the work of Michel Serres on multiple, connective intellection.

The connecting of ideas in the restless, dynamic, complex system, as emphasised by Morin, is a thoughtful activity, but thoughtful then far beyond mere rationality. Morin makes it explicit in his views on complex thinking. Michel Serres adds to this his view on thinking called 'connective intellection', or, 'multiple intellection'. Intellection does not only mean to act intelligently or with our intellect, but also to be intelligent or to be intellectual. Both the action and the being — of intelligence — are necessary for intelligence to excel. Intelligence is the translation of the Greek term *nous*, meaning mind or spirit, the origin of the terms noology and noosphere Morin uses.

The principles of multiple connective intellection are developed by Michel Serres in his five volumes on Hermes, the messenger of the gods, or to put it in a more worldly fashion 'the information messenger and interpreter' — the representative of all knowledge workers. Each principle, forming the subtitle of each volume in the Hermes series, is developed in the following separate books: Communication (in the sense of con-vers-ation) (Serres, 1969), Interference (also inter-reference) (Serres, 1972), Transduction (or translation) (Serres, 1974a), Distribution (also dissemination) (Serres, 1977a) and Passage (in the sense of ondular roads or pathways between the sciences, literature and philosophy) (Serres, 1980) (For the translation of essays from these sources, see Serres 1982b).

The thought experiences implied by these five principles assume a 'mutation of the cogito' (Crahay, 1988), that is a mutation of the ability of humans to know and to think only along the lines of traditional conceptions of knowing and thinking towards new and different ways. The core issues that are relevant for this article are cleverly and concisely summarised by Jean Ladrière (1988). This other cogito, this ability to know and to think differently, should be cultivated and put to work by all working in the knowledge field and living in the so-called information or knowledge society. This is the best, the only primary, equipment or capability we have. All else is of secondary importance, not to say for one moment that they are not of great importance in their own way and their own domains of application. But what is of decisive importance is that the focus is placed on the special mental, spiritual, thinking capacities of humans that respond to a multi-dimensional conception of knowledge. These views will be elaborated under the theme of the thoughtful methodology of Michel Serres as an acritical anti-method consisting of multiple, connective intellection or thought.

Both these thinkers are adamant about the shortcomings of the traditional methodological approaches. Serres (1997: 136) writes: 'We have at our disposal tools, notions, and efficacy, in great numbers; we lack on the other hand, an intellectual sphere free of all relations of dominance. Many truths, very little goodness. A thousand certainties, rare moments of invention.' Compare in this regard also his remarks on method when he states that repeating a method is profoundly boring and nothing but a kind of laziness. He writes: 'Who is more profoundly boring than the repetitive reasoner who copies or seems to construct by constantly repositioning the same cube? Ruminating on the past – what a system? Repeating a method – what laziness! Method seeks but does not find' (Serres, 1997: 100). His views on method are summarised by Harari and Bell (1982: xxxvi) in the following appropriate way: 'The term method itself is problematic because it suggests the notion of repetition and predictability – a method that anyone can apply. Method implies also mastery and closure both of which are detrimental to invention. On the contrary Serres's method invents: it is thus an anti-method.' The application of the five principles is the condition for the two options. Method means literally to be on the road, a made road, with the implication that we can see only what is visible from the road and nothing else. In order to see more we have to leave the road and move away – 'off the beaten track'. The real exciting places are often to be found there.

Serres's acritical approach of 'multiple, collective intellection' is developed in a rich *oeuvre* of more than 40 books, dealing with themes like science, knowledge, humans, information, ecology, foundations and so forth. But for the purposes of this chapter I wish to concentrate on his five books already mentioned on the philosophy of information, organised around the theme of the wing-footed messenger-god of the Greeks, namely Hermes. These publications have specific relevance for information and the thinking about information and knowledge, information messages and communication, and information work, with strong suggestions about the research endeavours related to these themes and sub-themes. Let us never forget that methodology, despite the fact that it relates to the work of research, is always, without any exception, also a work of thought (See Serres, 2008). That is why 'intellection' is such a central theme. It helps us to move beyond and away from the exclusivity and rigidities of traditional method and the blind spots created by it towards a more comprehensive approach. This will hopefully become clear when one attends to these publications.

The role of the knowledge worker is not to conquer a territory, but to attempt 'to see at a large scale, to be in full possession of a multiple and sometimes connected intellection' (Serres, 1980: 24). This remark calls for an explanation. 'To see at a large scale' implies a notion of space, and specifically in our case the space(s) of knowledge – not only single books but the whole of the library! There are at least two different views of space. One is that science has convinced us that in the classification of the spaces of knowledge the local was included in the global and that a path always existed between the two. This assumption implied a homogeneous space of knowledge ruled by a single scientific or universal truth that guaranteed the validity of the passage. There is, however, a qualitatively different perspective on space, namely that a more complex space can be envisaged. In such a space the passage from one local singularity to another would always require an arduous effort.

*Rather than a universal truth, in the more complex case one would have a kind of truth that functions only in pockets, a truth that is always local, distributed haphazardly in a plurality of spaces. The space of knowledge ... would not be homogeneous or rigidly bound together, it would be 'in tatters'.*

*(Harari & Bell, 1982: xiii)*

Serres writes:

*No, the real is not cut up into regular patterns, it is sporadic, spaces and times with straits and passes ... Therefore I assume there are fluctuating tatters; I am looking for the passage among these complicated cuttings. I believe, I see that the state of things consists of islands sown in archipelagos on the noisy, poorly understood disorder of the sea ... the emergence of sporadic rationalities that are not evidently or easily linked. Passages exist, I know, I have drawn some of them in certain works using certain operators ... (1980: 23–4, own translation)*

From this point of view it is clear: the truth is that the universality of a model is not possible. 'What is evident on the contrary is the cohabitation of different systems of thought (hence of multiple models and truths) which form any number of unique discourses, each justified by a set of chosen coordinates and by underlying presuppositions' (Harari & Bell, 1982: xiv). Rigour and coherence are regional. Universality and the global can for this very reason only be conceived in a mode that recognises the predominance of regionality and the local. Serres writes:

*Each domain in its own systematicity circulates an autonomous type of truth; each domain has a philosophy of the relations of its truth to its system and of the circulation along these relations. In addition, it exhibits unique types of openings onto other domains that make it a regional epistemology of the system of science. ... One must resolutely open a new epistemological spectrum and read the colours that our prejudices had previously erased. Logic contains one theory of science (or several), but mathematics surely contains another one, and most likely several. Information theory is consciously developing one also... In this coherent but open world, each province is a world and has a world, so that epistemology ... becomes pluralised and relativised within the system. (1972: 31–2, own translation)*

To see on a large scale *means* to understand that the foundation of knowledge presupposes neither one philosophical discourse, nor one scientific discourse, but only regional epistemologies. The connection and connectivity between the epistemologies become important. To see on a large scale, in other words to see in terms of multiplication, regionalisation, localisation, *means* also to attempt to travel through as much space as possible, searching for passages between the different spaces. The notion of seeing brings us in contact with the word 'theory' which can also in an etymological sense be linked to seeing. The word 'intellection' means also to see with the mind's eye, that is it is an intellectual, thoughtful activity – the knowledge worker as thinker in this way is always able to see new things, new solutions to problems, new options, which means that they are those people able to invent.

This journey of Serres through multiple times, spaces and cultural formations suggests the contours of a *general programme* which Harari and Bell (1982) outline for us. Serres' personal itinerary takes us through many thinkers and disciplines so that we may conclude: his itinerary is encyclopaedic, covering the three great modes of knowledge (spaces): the philosophic, the scientific and the mythic (or literature). His encyclopaedic concerns (for our purposes since many books have been published by him after this period) are expressed in the five volumes of the Hermes series already mentioned. In addition *The Parasite* (2007) deals with the conditions for an epistemology of human relations which we can hardly stay without. In the Hermes series Serres indicates and demonstrates the connections, the multiplicity, the intellection, the passages between science, philosophy and myth (fiction) that can be achieved when a Hermes-style of knowledge work can be pursued. A pursuit of this style and nature will be much more fruitful than the standard approaches we play around with and which imply not much more than a vague hope that we may have success in finding something.

In this regard the little book by Crahay (1988) on Serres will be especially significant and includes a most significant preface by Jean Ladrière (1988: 9−15). 'A new space of understanding' is opened up for us by the meditations of Michel Serres,' writes Ladrière (1988: 15). The thought of Michel Serres is a thought of multiple entries (Ladrière, 1988: 14). We ourselves can explore other roads, opening in front of us ... possible spaces. Every text of Serres in their inter-crossings with the others become revelatory for all the others and in the process they tell us of the circulation of meaning. It is therefore only by a reading operating in several registers at the same time, attentive at every instance to the references, to the relations, to the connections, to the correspondents, to the convergences, to the effect of mutual symbolisation, to the outbursts and the polymorph of significations, that one can truly enter into their mode of significance. It is a call for a mode of reading that Serres himself via Bruno Latour would recommend: an acritical reading. He articulates the multiple and contrasting voices of our strange culture. He allows us (perhaps even invites us) to follow multiple roads (ondulary roads). He opens the way to 'a true poematics of nature. We are thus on a way (achemine) to such a point that the thought of form and of morphogenesis become the thought of meaning, of the verb, of freedom, and at the end of the event' (Ladrière, 1988: 15, my translation). Note the important focus on form and morphogenesis, the creation of form, so immensely relevant in the context of information work as the work of form-giving, the spiritual partner of meaning-giving.

We find in Serres' understanding of the knowing mind 'a mutation of the cogito' and this mutation needs to be carefully articulated, especially because of its implication for our understanding of thinking (multiple, connective intellection). This means the end of a philosophy of representation and the beginning of 'a pluralist logic'. This reinterpretation of the cogito rests on 'a thought of forms' that exchanges representation for interference (see Serres, 1972). We also find Serres using all the familiar philosophical terms, such as cogito, subject, but displaced in a subtle way so that a new philosophy gradually emerges that signifies by way of interferences and not by way of projection or of representation. For example:

> *The COGITO becomes a fragmented, intermittent, erring, and contingent cogito; the subject is no longer a fixed point, it is nothing but circulation; the object escapes representation; thinking is no longer representation but pure movement; logos becomes a pluralist logos; being is no longer substance but made up of appearances, of events, of encounters, of relations, of qualities, of meaning; the*

*infinite remains undetermined; the ontological reality remains undifferentiated chaos, mixed multiplicities; and philosophy is the tacit place of welcome where all roads come together, get mixed and melt into one another like the centre of a star and method is only the story of voyages. (Ladrière, 1988: 13−14, my translation)*

We are looking for an image of a thinking that does not represent.

*Outside the fixedness of representation thinking is to move from one structure of representation to another, to a flow that connects different structures, and different spaces. To think is to connect and to disconnect circulations, to cross in all senses the transcendental space of communication, to intercept and exchange forms and structures in this space − each structure operates a crossing and exchanges. The subject, the ego of the cogito, is no longer a fixed point; it is nothing but circulation; being circulation.*

*(Crahay, 1988: 73−4, my translation)*

Finally, four book-length studies on four authors, each in his own way a system builder and in whose work scientific thought plays an important role, offer an acute illustration of Leibniz (see Serres, 1982a), Jules Verne (see Serres, 1974b), Zola (see Serres, 1975) and Lucretius (see Serres, 1977b), although the main focus of their work is the humanities. Serres made a study of these authors simply to illustrate his idea of 'seeing on a grand scale, multiple and sometimes connective intellection' since this is what is really relevant for us today and this is exactly what these authors have been doing. Be on the outlook in these works for terms like multiplicity, connection and connectivity, seeing on a grand scale, in other words, crossing spaces and following passages from the sciences to myth and back again. The important element of these studies is that they show us to what extent these authors establish links between the sciences and fiction or myth and at the same time combine and stitch together these efforts in a qualitative way by making use of very thoughtful philosophical inputs, inputs that are unavoidable despite our anxious efforts to deny their importance and to avoid them altogether. Because we are human we cannot help but think. Since we have to think in any case let us try and make the best of it by starting to think inventively. It will be useful to read Harari and Bell (1982: xv−xxx) for a fuller understanding of the contribution of these authors and how they are following passages from the sciences to myth and back again.

## 6.4 Conclusion

In order for us to be solid knowledge workers and sound researchers in our field, it will be important to follow Morin and Serres on their exciting journeys through the fullness of reality and the knowledges of reality with the help of a special kind of thinking adequate for this purpose of getting real access to this fullness. Let us think along the lines suggested by these two giants. We will not be mistaken by following this route, nor will our clients be disappointed. They look for solutions; they look for something new.

The brief discussion of each of them gave us a feeling for the thoughtful activity, beyond mere rationality and its one-dimensional thinking that is required from us if we want to come to terms and explore fully 'the information society as a dynamic and restless system', or the domains of complexity sketched by Morin. Unless we cultivate our capacity of intellection we will forever linger on the edges of this society, called the knowledge society, without really gaining access to its richness, wealth and excitements. We will never share in the adventures it offers and the solutions it promises. When we say that we need more than reason alone we mean that we need full human intelligence, human spirituality, to be brought into the picture, and by implication wisdom – going far beyond calculation as the computer scientist, Weizenbaum (1984), suggested long ago. In this respect we should take heed of the urgent message of a figure like George Steiner (1998) with his 'barbarism of ignorance' together with the possibility that developments in our times are stripping us of knowledge and bring about, despite our cleverness, a stupidity and an ignorance that may eventually destroy us if we take Isabelle Stengers (2009) seriously with her analyses of the time of catastrophe and barbarism that may be forthcoming. In addition to this we may include the significant study by Jean-Pierre Dupuy (2002) on the same theme.

These are articulations of the challenges we have to face that will be more than demanding and require immense inputs from us to save ourselves and the generations to come. In case these challenges are really of such immense proportions as people predict we will need very special abilities to cope. Mere skills will be totally inadequate. Only the best humans can offer in terms of multiple intellection, noological finesse and emotional, moral and spiritual capacity will be good enough for us to cope – hopefully. In this regard, see Chapter 4.

The notions of re-enchantment of spirituality (Griffiths, 1988a), the re-enchantment of science (Griffiths, 1988b), the re-enchantment of the world (Stengers 2000; Stiegler & Ars Industrialis, 2006) and the re-invention of spirituality (Stiegler & Ars Industrialis, 2006) are brought forward as urgent appeals directed to us from various sources and directions to come to terms with the dreadful spirit of our times, that affect our scientific work, our managerial practices, our research endeavours, our strategies, visions and policies of knowledge work that we must develop if we want to survive and not collapse into a state of barbarism and catastrophe. These re-enchantments are stitched together and if engaged in wholeheartedly, which can only happen through multiple, connective intellection with noological and noospheric inspirations, will represent our ability to establish new links and connections. All new connections bring forward new things, dispositions, strategies, plans because they are constantly driven and guided by new ideas. This is our guarantee, the only guarantee of inventing a liveable future for the human race.

Information scientists and information workers are the best situated to pursue these comprehensive challenges in terms of sound informatisation endeavours. We are connected in a special way to the pool of knowledge, insight and wisdom. The most fateful thing that can happen is that 'we may get into the position of losing knowledge' (Naccache, 2010) unless we comply wholeheartedly with these challenges. This also would be our only effective resistance against the possible advent of an immensely threatening barbarism (Stengers, 2009).

# References

Atlan, H. (1986). *Entre le cristal et la fumée: Essai sur l'organisation du vivant.* Paris: Seuil.

Bachelard, G. (1934). *Le nouvel esprit scientifique.* Paris: Alcan.

Bernardis, M.-A., & Hagene, B. (1995). *Mesures & démesure.* Paris: La Cité des Sciences et de l'Industrie.

Blair, D. (2003). Information retrieval and the philosophy of language. *Annual Review of Information Science and Technology, 37,* 3–50.

Blair, D. (2006). Wittgenstein, language and information:'Back to the rough ground'. Dordrecht: Springer.

Bohm, D., & Peat, F. D. (1989). *Science, order and creativity.* London: Routledge.

Bourdieu, P. (1996). Understanding. *Theory, culture and society, 13*(2), 17–37.

Bourdieu, P. (2001). *Science de la science et réflexivité.* Paris: Éditions Raisons d'agir.

Bourdieu, P., Chamboredon, J.-C., & Passeron, J.-C. (1991). *The craft of sociology: Epistemological preliminaries.* New York: Walter de Gruyter.

Crahay, A. (1988). *Michel Serres: la mutation du cogito.* Brussels: De Boeck-Wesmael.

Dupuy, J.-P. (1990). *Ordres et désordres: enquête sur un nouveau paradigme.* Paris: Seuil.

Dupuy, J.-P. (2002). *Pour un catastrophisme éclairé: quand l'impossible est certain.* Paris: Seuil.

Ekeland, I. (1988). *Mathematics and the unexpected.* Chicago: Chicago University Press.

Feyerabend, P. (1977). *Against method.* London: New Left Books.

Feyerabend, P. (1985). *Science in a free society.* London: Verso.

Fortin, R. (2008). *Penser avec Edgar Morin: lire La méthode.* Quebec: Les Presses de L'Université Laval.

Frohmann, B. (1994). Discourse analysis as a research method in library and information science. *Library and Information Science Research, 16*(2), 119–138.

Frohmann, B. (2001). Discourse and documentation: Some implications for pedagogy and research. *Journal of Education for Library and Information Science, 42*(1), 12–26.

Frohmann, B. (2004). *Deflating information: From science studies to documentation.* Toronto: Toronto University Press.

Gibbons, M., Limoges, C., Nowotny, H., Schwartzman, S., Scott, P., & Trow, M. (1994). *The new production of knowledge: The dynamics of science and research in contemporary societies.* London: Sage.

Griffiths, D. R. (Ed.), (1988a). *The Re-enchantment of science* New York: State University of New York Press.

Griffiths, D. R. (Ed.), (1988b). *Spirituality and society: Post-modern visions* New York: State University of New York Press.

Hacking, I. (Ed.), (1981). *Scientific revolutions* Oxford: Oxford University Press.

Harari, J. V., & Bell, D. F. (1982). Introduction: *Journal à plusieurs voies.* In M. Serres (Ed.), *Hermes: Literature, science, philosophy.* Baltimore, MD: Johns Hopkins University Press.

Husserl, E. (1970). *The crisis of european sciences and transcendental phenomenology.* Evanston, IL: Northwestern University Press.

Kuhlen, R. (1986). *Informationslinguistik.* Tübingen: Max Niemeyer Verlag.

Kuhlen, R. (2004a). *Informationsethik: Umgang mit Wissen und Information in elektronischen Raumen.* Konstanz: UVK Verlagsgesellschaft.

Kuhlen, R. (2004b). Informationsethik. In R. Kuhlen, T. Seeger, & D. Strauch (Eds.), *Grundlagen von Information und Dokumentation.* Munich: K.G. Sauer Verlag.

Ladrière, J. (1988). A new space of understanding. In A. Crahay (Ed.), *Michel Serres: La mutation du cogito*. Brussels: De Boeck-Wesmael.

Latour, B., & Woolgar, S. (1986). *Laboratory Life: The Construction of Scientific Facts*. Princeton, NJ: Princeton University Press.

Monod, J. (1979). *Chance and necessity*. London: Collins Fount Paperbacks.

Morin, E. (1977). *La méthode: 1. La nature de la nature*. Paris: Seuil.

Morin, E. (1980). *La méthode: 2. La vie de la vie*. Paris: Seuil.

Morin, E. (1983). Social paradigms of scientific knowledge. *SubStance, 39*, 3−20.

Morin, E. (1986). *La méthode: 3. La connaissance de la connaissance*. Paris: Seuil.

Morin, E. (1990a). *Introduction à la pensée complexe*. Paris: ESF éditeur.

Morin, E. (1990b). *Science avec Conscience*. Paris: Seuil.

Morin, E. (1991). *La méthode: 4. Les Idées: leur habitat, leur vie, leurs mœurs, leur organisation*. Paris: Seuil.

Morin, E. (2001). *La méthode: 5. L'humanité de l'humanité: l'Identité humaine*. Paris: Seuil.

Morin, E. (2004). *La méthode: 6. Éthique*. Paris: Seuil.

Naccache, L. (2010). *Perdons-nous connaissance?* Paris: Odile Jacob.

Nowotny, H., Scott, P., & Gibbons, M. (2004). *Re-thinking Science: Knowledge and the Public in the Age of Uncertainty*. Oxford: Polity Press.

Serres, M. (1969). *Hermès I: La communication*. Paris: Minuit.

Serres, M. (1972). *Hermès II: L'interférence*. Paris: Minuit.

Serres, M. (1974a). *Hermès III: La traduction*. Paris: Minuit.

Serres, M. (1974b). *Jouvences: Sur Jules Verne*. Paris: Minuit.

Serres, M. (1975). *Feux et signaux de brume: Zola*. Paris: Grasset.

Serres, M. (1977a). *Hermès IV: La distribution*. Paris: Minuit.

Serres, M. (1977b). *La naissance de la physique dans le texte de Lucrèce*. Paris: Minuit.

Serres, M. (1980). *Hermès V: Passage du Nord-Ouest*. Paris: Minuit.

Serres, M. (1982a). *Le système de Leibniz et ses modèles mathématiques*. Paris: PUF.

Serres, M. (1982b). Hermes: Literature, Science, Philosophy. Baltimore, MD: Johns Hopkins University Press.

Serres, M. (1995). *Conversations on science, culture and time*. Ann Arbor, MI: University of Michigan Press.

Serres, M. (1997). *The troubadour of knowledge*. Ann Arbor, MI: University of Michigan Press.

Serres, M. (2007). *The parasite*. Minneapolis, MN: University of Minnesota Press.

Serres, M. (2008). *The five senses: A philosophy of mingled bodies*. London: Continuum Books.

Steiner, G., & Spire, A. (1998). *Barbarie de l'ignorance: Collection conversations*. Latresne: Le bord de l'eau.

Stengers, I. (1997). *Power and Invention: Situating Science*. Minneapolis, MN: University of Minnesota Press.

Stengers, I. (2000). *The invention of modern science*. Minneapolis, MN: University of Minnesota Press.

Stengers, I. (2006). *La vierge et le neutrino: les scientifiques dans la tourmente*. Paris: Seuil.

Stengers, I. (2009). *Au temps des catastrophes: Résister à la barbarie qui vient*. Paris: La Découverte.

Stengers, I. (2013). *Une autre science est possible! Manifeste pour un ralentissement de sciences*. Paris: La Découverte.

Stengers, I., & Schlanger, J. (1991). *Les concepts scientifiques*. Paris: Gallimard.

Stiegler, B., & Ars Industrialis (2006). *Réenchanter le monde: la valeur esprit contre le populisme industriel.* Paris: Flammarion.

Weizenbaum, J. (1984). *Computer power and human reason: From judgment to calculation.* Harmondsworth: Pelican Books.

Wersig, G. (1990). The changing role of knowledge in an information society. In D. J. Foskett (Ed.), *The information environment: A world view.* New York: Elsevier Science.

# Let the new knowledge come: the atlas of knowledges

**7**

## 7.1 Introduction

It is interesting to note that for some time now the expression 'knowledge society' has been bandied about, referring to this particular time in history as if the concept were something totally new. South Africa's Draft White Paper on Higher Education (1997) is an example of how knowledge society is used. Another more recent international example is the Unesco World Report, *Towards Knowledge Societies* (2005). This report was the formal document for a world summit on the knowledge society in Tunisia. The approach of this document was severely and thoroughly criticised by Stiegler and Ars Industrialis (2006) on the basis of both a shallow conception of knowledge and serious misunderstanding about the nature of the social as reflected in the document. The first example refers to the South African society as 'a knowledge-driven and knowledge-dependent society' (Draft White Paper on Higher Education, 1997: 9) and stated unequivocally that 'in the context of the communications and information revolution, the social sciences and the humanities must contribute to the development of the analytic, intellectual, cultural and ethical skills and competencies necessary for participation in the knowledge society' (Draft White Paper on Higher Education, 1997: 6). It is nevertheless noteworthy that this phrase emerges at a stage when we are still in the process of debating the sense of referring to our time and age as the information age or the information society. Strangely enough it is also happening at a stage when the social sciences to some extent, but the humanities in particular, have landed in a situation of discredit where they have to fight for their right to exist and their future is under severe threat. Some contradiction is to be detected: they have to make contributions while their very existence is under threat.

But is it not true that knowledge has always been important? At no stage in human history can it be said that knowledge was less important than at any other stage. Human civilisations through the ages have in an undeniable way been characterised as being involved with knowledge. All major religions emphasise the crucial importance of knowledge. No knowledge means no civilisation, no religion, no progress and prosperity, no development and no life, no food and no health or even sanity. Knowledge is, as always, important in a very comprehensive sense. And it is still of decisive importance right now. No wonder that the famous German thinker, Hans-Georg Gadamer (1996: 16) refers to our 'absolute moral duty-to-know to the highest degree reasonable'.

Information Science as an Interscience.

Gadamer emphasises not only fractions of knowledge, bits and pieces, but knowledge in its fullness. In addition, a low level of reflection on methods of knowledge creation and development reveals both a certain methodological poverty and suggests the newness of a position of 'beyond-method', adequate for the fullness of knowledge as it becomes clear from his major work, *Truth and Method* (Gadamer, 1975) (see Chapter 4). Moreover, it needs to be emphasised that knowledge is in the last analysis a moral issue as well: it is our moral duty to know. In fact, during the last decades it has become a crucial question in certain circles whether knowledge is not secondary to ethics. The core of the thought of Levinas on this is clear: knowledge is an important product of the ethical situation itself and has tremendous ethical significance.

The identities, themes, reflections and reasons of knowledge occur within the exorbitant context of the non-identifiable, non-representable, non-thematisable, non-reflective, unjustified proximity of one face to another (Levinas, 1984, 1985). Felix Guattari (1995) with his 'ethico-aesthetic paradigm' emphasises, from a totally different perspective, the same insight. The fact that it is not the case in practice may explain on the one hand the many knowledge projects which lead to nothing, but also the manipulative abuse of knowledge with regard to both humans and nature. On the other hand, it may also explain the unconscious realisation that only knowledge in its fullness can bring about conditions favourable for humans and societies to live in. Out of this realisation emerges the need to collectively emphasise, as if it is something new, what should be self-evident: the all-importance of knowledge.

## 7.2    Reasons for such an emphasis on knowledge

What are the reasons for this emphasis on knowledge as if it is something altogether new, especially at present?

### 7.2.1   Awareness of the importance of knowledge

In the first place a general awareness of the vital importance of knowledge for individuals, institutions and societies seems to be emerging. More and more people are called upon to become involved in learning about and producing more and new forms of knowledge. Knowledge management has suddenly become a fashionable topic, almost a profession in its own right. The whole business world is taken up by knowledge management, intellectual capital, for instance. Many publications have seen the light during the past decade or more on this theme. We indeed find a rediscovery of the idea of the importance of knowledge for all sectors of society. It is important though to realise the nature of the conception of knowledge that is embraced and promoted in this context.

### 7.2.2   Development of electronic media

In the second place, what makes this phrase really fashionable is the development of electronic media, more specifically computers and their role in the knowledge sector. All of a sudden knowledge centres are found everywhere as if there is something really new for which centres have to be created. If not replacing libraries or creating institutions additional to libraries, these institutions are in many cases nothing but rebaptised libraries. In other words, libraries as knowledge centres are not new, but what is currently happening to libraries is fundamentally new. Knowledge networks, knowledge space and cyberspace and what these terms represent are to be integrated into this new conception of libraries as knowledge spaces or centres.

A new culture, called cyberculture (Lévy, 2001), is being developed. Characteristic of cyberculture is its emphasis on virtuality and virtual reality (Castells, 1997; Lévy, 1998), knowledge space and cyberspace (Lévy, 1997) and the post-human and the cyborg (Gray, 1995; Haraway, 1991; Hayles, 1999). These are not merely fashionable, but also seriously debatable terms. These terms are redescribing the world in which we live, but also who we are ourselves and what we can expect from knowledge. The differentiation between the real world and virtual worlds is not simply based on mind games. These expressions contain something new, something for us to explore if we want to understand our present world (Barrau & Nancy, 2011; Nancy, 1997, 2007; Virilio, 2001). Understanding the present is one of the most important challenges we have to cope with. Post-human and cyborg together with 'the age of spiritual machines' (Kurzweil, 2000) are not merely hollow and empty expressions either. They imply a redescription of and reconfiguration of humans and human subjectivity which has been expertly articulated by Morin (2001) and Serres (2001). All of us, whether in science, in art or in religion, willy-nilly still cling to an archaic, long outdated understanding of human subjectivity, the Cartesian one. In this idiom the human subject is a self-assured being, in control of itself and its world and fully aware of its own identity. This perspective is so much a part of us that it is almost second nature and as if it is of our own making so that we no longer know where it comes from. This is now subject to serious and definite revision as was mentioned, also very specifically with a view to human bodiliness in the age of computers and technology (Hillis, 1999; Ihde, 2002; Nancy, 2000; Serres, 1999).

Compare the imposing study of technique and technology in the volumes by Bernard Stiegler, five of which are intended with three already published (1994, 1996, 2001), to mention one example as an articulation of this new knowledge culture in which a number of themes are explored or are meant to be explored: the invention of the human; thinking, technical thinking and the future; the genesis of disorientation; the future of spirituality; the bad state of education and teaching; images and imagination and many more. The work done by Pierre Lévy (1993, 1997, 1998, 2001) is another example. He addresses in a comprehensive way issues such as the future of human thinking in the age of informatics, collective intelligence and the anthropology of cyberspace, virtuality and cyberculture and its implications for understanding knowledge in a comprehensive way. The study of Latour (1996) on the love of technology should be added here. The publication series on *Electronic Mediations* under the editorship of Hayles, Poster and Weber is a further example and a number of significant volumes have already been published: Hillis (1999) on digital sensations, identity and embodiment; Rutsky (1999) on high tech, art and the post-human; Poster (2001) on the internet; Ihde (2002) on bodies in technology; and Lévy (2001) on cyberculture. Spinner's study on 'the order of knowledge in the age of information' is an equally impressive series on the same issues (Spinner, 1994). There are many more.

What we encounter here is the development of a unique knowledge domain, referred to and developed as knowledge space, a quite unique anthropological space. It is a virtual space, a space without limits and boundaries. All knowledge forms become relevant and impact on every other. Compare in this regard a variety of studies on the Internet from various perspectives such as its threats and promises and essence as well as questions of control: Graham (1999), Shapiro (1999), Breton (2000) and Poster (2001). Texts, even the most sacred as well as the most methodologically rigorous, no longer have any closure or finality and become impregnated by many others. Indeed, here is something new which we encounter − and it gives an impetus to the first very general point.

It will be extremely costly for us to stand on the sidelines, remaining spectators without exploring what is happening under our noses without taking it seriously, or taking these studies seriously only insofar as they fit in with the generation of a few new skills without any specific serious effort to understand. It is exciting to send messages worldwide, but the assumption is that the receivers have the vocabulary to understand what we send. It is fine to emphasise the importance of knowledge networks, but what is the use of these networks if we cannot interpret, understand and unravel what appears on our screens? Lack of understanding of these developments may have serious negative implications. Pierre Lévy (1998: 85) writes: 'I am convinced that the suffering that arises from submitting to virtualization without understanding it is one of the major causes of the madness and violence of our time.'

But these developments did not happen in a vacuum.

### 7.2.3   Intensive thought on the knowledge issue

I think the *third* reason why there is talk about a knowledge society in a new way is that the knowledge issue has been rethought lately on a grand scale altogether independent of these technical developments. Positivism and the positive, representation and stagnation of the methods used have been questioned in a thorough way (Colebrook, 2000). 'Let the new knowledge come', was formulated by Michel Serres (1989a) almost as a plea, an urge with a view to the emergence or development of alternatives. It seems to be a very general experience. During a recent overseas visit one of the themes colleagues abroad wanted as a contribution out of a number of choices was 'Let the new knowledge come'. Serres relates this new knowledge to a break with the sole focus on reason and rationality. Reason has optimally landscaped the earth until it has become stagnant, monotone and death-like in its absolute stability and totality. Here Serres sees reality experienced exclusively as rationality. In the guise of fables, parables and stories, Serres (1995a) tells us about the creative vivacity of multiples and fuzzy mixtures in which he comes to terms with what he calls the curse inherent in a singular, linear view of the earth, the perfect realisation of our mastery over the world. Once we understand multiple origins we also understand that this new knowledge breaks with the ranks of the rationalism of modern philosophy, world views and the culture of critisism. The new knowledge is comfortable with notions such as the indefinable, the unlimited and the uncertain. It is clear: plenty of intellectual energy is spent worldwide in a spontaneous way on this effort to elaborate on the comprehensive meaning of the word 'knowledge'. A fine collection of essays that illustrates the intensity and comprehensiveness of the debates in this regard has been published in a special issue of the journal *SubStance*, 22 (2/3) (1993), under the theme 'epistemocritique'.

## 7.3   Inflationary knowledge abuse

At a stage where there is, in certain circles where knowledge is high on the agenda, more talk about knowledge than ever before, reflection on the real nature of knowledge is almost entirely absent. It is not impossible that it is precisely the case at this stage that knowledge is less available and understood than ever before despite all this talk about knowledge. More use but less meaning and value signifies real inflationary knowledge abuse. For the first time the importance of knowledge is written into official documents on higher education. At the same time knowledge is taken for granted as if everybody simply knows what is understood by the term in the wealth of its nuances.

Is it not true that we hear more than ever before the little phrase uttered almost in total desperation: 'I do not understand', or perhaps even worse, 'it is too difficult'. There is no real disciplined effort to understand — hardly any focused application of the mind to what is to be understood.

Understanding is difficult to achieve and requires time, devotion, patience and deliberate input. Students and other readers often say that, but what they actually mean is that they are not really willing even to try and understand. One has, of course, to be convinced of the importance of understanding. Anything that requires effort or exertion to be understood in our time is not supposed to be. In an age of take-aways we are all satisfied or will be satisfied with knowledge take-aways as long as they carry our favourite flavour. Our societies are built on ready-made packages which require only a minimum amount of understanding. Just as we are working on a subsistence economy so too are we also extending the notion to knowledge — a subsistence economy of knowledge. We settle for the minimum needed to survive and are wary of too much.

What one finds manifested here is something very similar to what Shosana Felman (1987) in her study of Jacques Lacan characterised as 'the will to ignorance'. This will to ignorance is not a mere subjective and passive disposition — a matter of mere forgetfulness. It is actively pursued as well. The will to ignorance constructs barriers — barriers to method, barriers to theory, barriers to understanding, barriers to thinking. Of course, it is also related to the inability to know all, to have absolute knowledge, in the sense that it hides behind these impossibilities as a handy excuse.

There are deliberate efforts and strategies to promote this 'will to ignorance'. Can we distinguish between non-philosophical and philosophical notions of knowledge as some such as Alavi and Leidner (2001) would like to claim — and simply look at the philosophical from a distance? They stated explicitly:

> *It is unnecessary for purposes of this paper (on conceptual foundations of knowledge management by the way) to engage in a debate to probe, question, or reframe the term knowledge, or discover the 'universal truth' from the perspective of ancient and or modern philosophy. This is because such an understanding of knowledge was neither a determinant factor in building the knowledge-based theory of the firm nor in triggering researcher and practitioner interest in managing organizational knowledge.*
>
> *(Alavi & Leidner, 2001: 109)*

The interesting observation is that even they fall back on precisely the philosophy they rejected, which they clearly do not understand in the least, namely 'tacit' and 'explicit' knowledge borrowed from the philosopher Polanyi who published in the 1960s (Alavi & Leidner, 2001: 110). They even dare to philosophise about this philosophy. What is more — and I want to state it categorically — no conceptual foundations of or for anything, not even for knowledge management, can ever be un-philosophical or non-philosophical. It can only be bad philosophy. Only one more point: the better our philosophy the better and sounder our conceptual foundations.

Another strategy is the high premium placed on skills. Skills are extremely useful as long as they are kept in place. Reducing everything human to skills, even the so-called higher-order skills, contains serious threats in itself. In this sense skills offer a cul-de-sac; skills offer no perspective and are not meant to do so; skills are sterile with respect to inventive possibilities. There is a ceiling beyond which skills cannot take us; they do not have the capacity. All efforts to link serious human activities and endeavours to skills do not lift skills to new levels but bring down the human intellectual capacity to a lower level and block the full significance of any item such as life, thinking, people, management, method. Skills remain within a certain focus of human activity and cannot take over the full functions of thinking, life, people and so on. The moment this happens we try to make of these very unique human capabilities controllable entities. Absolute control means the absolute reduction of humans and ultimately dehumanisation. Heidegger (1968: 38) warns us 'to guard against the blind urge to snatch at a quick answer in the form of a formula' in an effort to answer the question: 'What is called thinking?' This warning is paraphrased by Ronell (1989: 26–7) in the following way:

> *The question of what is called thinking or of what does call for thinking must renounce access to an urge, an urge for blindness — the form of blindness that would permit us to 'snatch a quick answer in the form of a formula, a quick answer that would be graspable by the right kind of dialing system, preferably an automatic system.*

This suggestion, of course, is that we have to link the warning against this blindness to a warning against the blindness which promotes skills only at all costs.

The consequences of this abuse of knowledge by indulging in a caricature of knowledge (the refusal to use knowledge to the full, or to acknowledge its newness, or to link it to understanding) can be severe.

Let us attend to the implications for only a few directly relevant themes:

- Implications for *education: repetition versus invention*. The educational system creates memorisers instead of thinkers.
- The tragic developments in *organisational development* – never-ending reorganisation – with the minimum positive effect. More and more costly consultants are considered and less invention is promoted. The keenness and compulsiveness with which everybody is obliged to form part of this madness characterises all reorganisations. 'The cure for bad management is more management ... and this is the ultimate attempt to solve a crisis by escalation' (Illich, 1973: 9).
- Notice the confusion about the norms of and for *development* – development for whom, according to whom and in terms of whose views? People fail to grasp that underlying institutional structures most of the time 'escalate what they are meant to eliminate' (Illich, 1973: 8).
- See Lévy (1997: 3) with regard to totalitarianism: *totalitarianism collapsed ... [because] it was incapable of collective intelligence.* This is relevant for and applicable to all the points mentioned above and sheds considerable light on our approach to the age of knowledge.

The previous reference to Lévy (1998: 85) about violence and madness is certainly applicable to each of these examples. In line with the previous quote it can be stated in paraphrased form: 'I am convinced that the suffering that arises from *submitting* to *virtualisation* (also read education, management, development, societal reform) *without understanding* it is one of the major causes of the madness and violence of our time' (my emphasis). Madness and violence are so severe because they are due not only to one but to many issues together.


# 7.4    In pursuit of a new conception of knowledge

This can be promoted by addressing the parallel theoretical developments that promote inter-disciplinarity, the idea of the atlas of knowledges (Serres, 1994a) and knowledge networks (Parrochia, 2001) emerging from these developments, the reinvention and reorganisation of terminological issues that will enable knowledge workers to move around along the lines indicated by the atlas of knowledges, and consideration of intriguing knowledge relationships such as complexity, intelligence, thinking and communication.


## 7.4.1    Parallel theoretical developments

Apart from and in a sense parallel to the developments in the field of electronic media, the same issues have been extensively explored by theorists from different sectors of intellectual work. When Nelson (1980) emphasised the term 'hypertext' in the USA in the 1960s in the context of computer developments Kristeva (1980) developed the term 'intertext' in France against the background of the theory of literature also in the 1960s. Both these terms emphasise the links between texts, the one more technical and the other more theoretical. Many other theoretical developments brought forward the same issues and highlighted the same tendencies and dynamics: Derrida, Deleuze, Guattari, Lacan, Lyotard, Serres and others.

The agreements and the foci are so similar that it becomes impossible to keep the two strands of thought separate. Notions such as cyberculture, cyberspace, virtuality and knowledge networks, which are useful in a computer context, can in no way be adequately and properly developed or even assessed without complementary theoretical perspectives. It is significant that Michel Serres (2014) in a recent publication refers to his writings, in which 'the pursuit of new knowledge' is predominant, as 'hypertextual', by which he means that 'each text refers to others and inserts themselves in a more vast totality, exactly like in an informatic hypertext in which there is a series of links that refers to all the others in an almost infinite way' (my translation). These two domains are indispensable to each other and to an understanding of knowledge and information in its fullness. This is a particularly new, altogether new, domain of thinking, knowing and culture with its own characteristics, demands, challenges, threats and promises. Connections are possible. Excellent examples are Derridean reflection combined with Stiegler's research on the technical in the corporate sector; Deleuze's work on a thousand plateaus and Serres' work on knowledge networks fruitfully combined with Lévy's contributions from the sector of computer technology and programming. There are many others. Myerson (2001) with his discussion of Heidegger, Habermas and the mobile phone offers an excellent example. The mobility of knowledge, the crucial importance of understanding, a mobile vision of the world and new dimensions of communication are emphasised. What we find is actually the creation of a new knowledge domain, a new knowledge culture as it were. In this milieu the 'information multiplicities' emphasised by Johnstone (1998) and the 'noise of culture' in 'a world of information', discussed by Paulson (1988), start to make sense.

### 7.4.2    The newness of the new conception of knowledge

Michel Serres' philosophy of knowledge deserves more reading and attention than it receives and can be used as an example of the development of the new conception of knowledge. Against this background it is important to show that knowledge is a much more complex issue than our research endeavours and institutions, and more recently 'knowledge management companies', try to make out. All forms of knowledge are to be taken seriously. We humans are challenged to be inventively involved with the issue of knowledge. Knowledge (and not any deformations of it, and also not its disfigurement by powers such as rhetoric, or political systems and ideologies, or colonisations, or decolonisations, or even the market), and knowledge only, is the issue that can take us (the human race and human societies) forward in any sensible way. The last issue will be to emphasise these matters in such a way that it will form food for thought and further discussions.

The actor/network theory inspired by Michel Serres, the grounds of which were well articulated by him back in 1969 (*La communication*) as well as his core *oeuvre* rotating around the Hermes figure and his never-ending involvement with and indulgence in information, are all demonstrations of unlimited scope, the transgression of boundaries, the mobility of the nomad. Another perspective on globalisation, much more constructive and much less threatening than the economic/market version of globalisation, emerges in this view. This input is, however, not without intersection with the other. As a matter of fact a great deal they have in common are their links to electronic media. We should never forget that the theoretical perspectives developed with global implications were not in its initial stages inspired or supported by electronic media. As a latecomer to the scene it indeed reinforces, activates and intensifies these theoretical views immensely. One of the more recent publications by Serres, *Angels: A Modern Myth*, is a particularly relevant publication in this regard (Serres, 1994b). Here he re-emphasises in a very pertinent way how relevant the 'theory of the angels' is for the contemporary information society (Serres, 2014: 107−8).

Another *way* of making the same point is a reminder of Merleau-Ponty's view that meaning is like spots of light surrounded by rugged clouds of night, or glowing islands. This *oeuvre* articulates the web of meaning which can neither nihilistically deny light nor, at the same time, can it apocalyptically pretend that all we see is light and that there is no darkness. The recent debates about chaos, order and complexity are relevant here. Serres' Hermes philosophy (he published five books in his Hermes series) is about this.

> One of the most beautiful things that our era is teaching us is to approach with light and simplicity the very complex things previously believed to be the result of chance, of noise, of chaos, in their ancient sense of the word. Hermes, the messenger, first brings light to texts and signs that are 'hermetic', that is, obscure. A message comes through while battling against the background noise. Likewise, Hermes, traverses the noise, toward meaning.
>
> (Serres, 1995b: 65−6)

Some additional views, along similar lines, which make the self-sufficiency of our generally accepted views on knowledge ludicrous and highly questionable and therefore risky, are the following:

- Jean-François Lyotard (1988: 28), the philosopher, writes in *Peregrinations* about the importance of doing away with 'the delusion of consistency' (the attitude reflected in the so-called 'old knowledge') without shying away from the complexity of things. He writes: 'It is time to complicate a bit our approach by opening up gaps inside what is certainly a too thick cloud of thought in order to do away with the delusion of consistency and to make ourselves receptive again to more intricate events.'
- Hundertwasser, the artist, is even more explicit:

> In 1953 I realized that the straight line leads to the downfall of mankind. But the straight line has become an absolute tyranny. The straight line is something cowardly drawn with a rule, without thought or feeling; it is the line which does not exist in nature. And that line is the rotten foundation of our doomed civilization. Even if there

*are places where it is recognized that this line is rapidly leading to perdition, its course continues to be plotted ... Any design undertaken with the straight line will be stillborn. Today we are witnessing the triumph of rationalist know-how and yet, at the same time, we find ourselves confronted with emptiness. An aesthetic void, desert of uniformity, criminal sterility, loss of creative power. Even creativity is prefabricated. We have become impotent. We are no longer able to create. That is our real illiteracy.*

*(Hundertwasser, as quoted by Peitgen & Richter, 1986: v)*

- Mandelbrot, the geometrician, puts the same problem in a very clinical *way* in perspective when he writes:

  *Why is geometry often described as cold and dry? One reason lies in its inability to describe the shape of a cloud, a mountain, a coastline, or a tree. Clouds are not spheres, mountains are not cones, coastlines are not circles, and bark is not smooth, nor does lightning travel in a straight line ... Nature exhibits not simply a higher degree but an altogether different level of complexity. Note the number of distinct scales of length of patterns for all purposes infinite. The existence of these patterns challenges us to study those forms that Euclid leaves aside as being form-less, to investigate the morphology of the amorphous. Mathematicians have dis-dained this challenge, however, and have increasingly chosen to flee from nature by devising theories unrelated to anything we can see or feel. (1982: 12)*

- A fairly recent publication and exhibition in Paris on *Mesures et démesures* (*Measurement and the Unmeasurable*) (Bernardis & Hagene, 1995) demonstrates in various ways to what extent the measurable is not reliable and that our decisions, even scientific ones, are very often affected and directed by what cannot be measured. We should never be tempted to confuse knowledge with the measurement of knowledge. These two entities, although they are somewhat linked, are also incompatible.

These views cut deep into the heart of our knowledge culture and consequently our information culture, and calls for drastic revision, re-articulation and rethinking. This is exactly what Michel Serres has been doing for the past 30 years and is still working on currently. His works are, each of them in its own way, an effort − and a very successful effort − to articulate precisely these issues related to a new knowledge culture (cf., for example, the book by Assad (1999) in which she offers lively interpretations of and comments on some of his books).

Three general and very dominant features of his project of thinking that have an impact on all his other themes should also be mentioned and eventually explored: he is an *acritical* philosopher; he is also a philosopher of *networks* and *invention*. These three outstanding characteristics of his thinking determine the mode of his *oeuvre*. Each work stands in the light of an acritical inventiveness. Networks are enabling factors for inventions. This makes of his thinking something drastically different from the enlightenment philosophy.

### 7.4.3 The atlas of knowledges and world-mapping knowledge

These views introduce to us the idea of a road map for knowledges. (See the impressive book edited by Serres entitled *Elements d'Histoire des sciences*

(*Elements of the History of Science*) (Serres, 1989c) and also Serres (1994a).) This is the idea of giving or working on a comprehensive, all-inclusive map of the world of knowledge, which is at stake here.

The history of the thinking of Michel Serres is a history of wrestling with the issue of knowledge. All his books rotate around this theme and each one of them elaborates and highlights a particular perspective of this issue. Themes addressed by his many books include communication, translation, interference, distribution, passage, statues, the five senses, genesis, detachment, the hermaphrodite, Rome, the atlas and more are all woven around this formidable theme, so totally indispensable for the human race and at issue since the beginning of human history. Compare the history of religions and cultures and the role knowledge played all the time in all these cultural traditions. Knowledge and its importance for human life and existence is no new invention, least of all an invention of the sciences or of the marketplace. It is certainly not suddenly an important theme because it is surprisingly included in the rhetoric, vocabulary and marketing strategies of big companies, or finds a strategic place in organisational politics, or in business and management contexts where it has never been a prominent issue before.

Serres' deep, honest authentic urge at the end of his book *Detachment* (1989a), namely 'let the new knowledge come', eventually culminates in the statement in one of his later books, *Atlas* (1994a), in the following terms: 'We should no longer run after a knowledge universe, but pursue the multiplicity of possible knowledge worlds' (1994a: 276). In this book he unravels the zigzag tours and detours leading to an illuminating enlightening focal point where all routes converge in a single knot — harmonious, significant and meaningful This knot constantly requires to be untied. In his reflections on knowledge, information is never far behind and never left out of the picture. As a matter of fact it finds a very special place. Serres can indeed be called one of the most productive, imaginative and inventive philosophers of information. The implications will hopefully become clearer as we proceed.

We need an atlas to guide us through landscapes, cities and countries because without one we will easily get lost. Equally important is an atlas for the landscape of knowledge, and its place in culture and society, hence his exercise in mapping the world of knowledge as comprehensively as possible. Knowledge as map or atlas is needed in a much more comprehensive sense than merely for the purposes of physical moving around. Knowledge is the issue that enables us to find our way and direction through life. It is indispensable for us as living beings.

*Atlas* represents a more comprehensive and open-ended notion than *encyclopaedia*, which is closed and finite. This rethinking of knowledge in new terms is made necessary by the development of a new conception of knowledge, which emerged during past decades, with vast implications for the creation, dissemination, transmission and utilisation of knowledge for the well-being of individuals and society. These new developments also pose serious new challenges for the activity of thinking, the fantasia of thinking, and the pursuit of science in the sense of nomad science. Gilles Deleuze, a key thinker in these matters as has already been shown, incidentally had close connections with Serres.

As has already been emphasised, Serres prefers to speak of 'a multiplicity of possible knowledge worlds' rather than the classical 'knowledge universe', for very self-evident reasons (cf. also Serres, 1995a). These reasons became prominent in solid theoretical terms but were also supported by developments in the area of electronic media which certainly facilitate them. In this way human thinking is confronted with dramatic challenges. In a way similar to our talking of networks of roads (represented by the idea of the atlas) we can speak of networks in a more abstract sense, referring to the links between knowledges, institutions, insights and many other related issues (see Serres, 1972).

## 7.4.4   Knowledge and information space

At an early stage Serres developed his theory of networks of communication (*La communication*), which offers in itself a model of communication more adequate and significant than the linear model of Shannon and Weaver. This theory can be made fruitful for other linkages as well, very useful from the point of view of knowledge usage. We can easily detect from what has already been stated that the notion of space, real and/or virtual, is self-evidently suggested. Atlas, map and network are all spatial terms. Knowledge space and information space will become crucial issues in this regard – and very importantly so – as a space to be inhabited!

Real space implies that a road exists where one can indicate the exact departure point and point of destination. Virtual space, on the contrary, entails the following: 'If Hermes carries his messages only to a unique sender ... while Leibniz, like the Angels, describes the passages from whatever place towards the universe, or from this global point to such sojourn by virtual intermediaries, it becomes perfectly clear from where the idea to design these sheaves in world maps, in an Atlas, originated' (Serres, 1994a: 33). His whole *oeuvre* rotates around this theme: communication between the sciences, between knowledges, between the sciences and societies, and movement in all directions. For this reason the notion of space is important as well as mapping knowledges in this space. A brief look at his works will illustrate this. At the same time this way of articulating knowledges emphasises self-evidently the idea of a new knowledge that is not a given but should be pursued (Serres, 1989b).

Serres' notion of communication involves transfers from one science to another, or from the purest science to philosophy and even poetry. Communication traverses these spaces that would be much less clear and transparent than one would have believed. The titles of many of his books, like communication, interference, distribution, translation, north-west passages, lighthouses and fog horns suggest movement from place to place. Not things and operations but relations and rapports are what he is concerned about. A reading of his books may seem difficult since it is constantly a matter of changes and moves. This changing and these transformations and these wanderings either follow or invent the path of a relation, relations between the sciences, between knowledges, between humans and knowledges.

When one reviews them it will be possible to retrace easily how he passed from mathematics to physics, from physics to the life sciences and to the human sciences, without ever leaving behind the historical component. But these movements do not make up a seamless list which occupies a flat space. They suggest a hilly landscape, ondular pathways – chaotic and fractal, much closer to reality. Besides utilising concepts by which he wants to facilitate movement and communication in a successful way he also uses characters which also find expression in some of the titles of his books. Some of these characters are: Hermes, Parasite, Hermaphrodite, Harlequin, Troubadour of Knowledge. In these books where he meditates on successful communication, the difficulties, obstacles and conditions pertaining to transformations, movements, communications and translations are laid down in detail and make for fascinating and exhilarating reading.

A brief illustration of how Michel Serres in his books tries to establish relations not only between disciplines but also between ideas and relations as conditions of our knowledge creations and the world in which we live and which we create in some way should be sufficient. This may help us to understand a little better the idea of the atlas of knowledges, the idea of the urgency of a new conception of knowledge, and why a comprehensive world mapping of knowledges is required. How sociology is situated in astronomy (the two most distant sciences in terms of positivism's classification) is discussed in his *The Origins of Geometry* (see Serres, 1993). How politics is situated in physics is the great question of *The Natural Contract* (Serres, 1995c). How technology and physics are both situated in an anthropology of death is the main concern of *Statues* (see Serres, 1987a). The possibility of fitting together information theory, parasitology and table manners is discussed in *The Parasite* (see Serres, 2007). In his book on Zola (*Lighthouses and Fog Horns*) (see Serres, 1975) he situates thermodynamics with genetics and both of them with the history of religion. The question he tries to answer in *Hermaphrodite* (Serres, 1987b) is how it is possible to link the symmetry/ asymmetry of left and right, of orientation and of sense, in the physical and in the human sense of the word. These passages between the disciplines or sciences are explored in a very specific sense in *The North-West Passage* (see Serres, 1980) and strongly recommended for teaching in *The Troubadour of Knowledge* (Serres, 1997). Nothing can be more relevant for knowledge and information workers – we simply have to undertake these journeys and do that on a continuous basis. This is a demanding challenge, but hardly anything can be more rewarding at the same time.

## 7.4.5 Trees of knowledges

The very rich and productive insights of Michel Serres, as discussed up till now, are in a very significant way 'operationalised' by Authier and Lévy (1996). They do this under the theme of 'trees of knowledges'. According to them the knowledge system should be dealt with in terms of its principles as well as its effects. They have fruitfully applied the philosophic insights of Serres in an economic and business sense. Their focus in this regard on knowledge and intelligence deserves attention.

Intelligence incorporates a collective dimension: it is not only languages and institutions that think in us, but the whole of the human world, with its lines of desire, affective polarities, hybrid mental machines and landscapes of meaning paved with images. To act on one's environment, no matter how slightly, even on a purely technological material or physical level means that we erect a shared world that thinks differently in each of us, indirectly secrete some subjective quality, work in and with affect. By living, acting and thinking, we weave the very fabric of the life of others. For this reason human communities can be said to be intelligent in a collective sense. A common space is created where the effects of these ideas on individuals, on enterprises and employers in general, and on teachers and educationalists, are immense in the drive to the creation of a new civility (see Authier & Lévy, 1996).

Collective intelligence thinks in us. We can take individual pleasure in the collective intelligence, which enhances and modifies our own intelligence but at the same time enhances the creation of intelligent communities.

## 7.5   The necessity for embracing the new knowledge culture

The resolve should be to overcome the devastating negative consequences of inflationary knowledge abuse as discussed earlier in section 7.3, and to achieve a full embracement of the new knowledge culture as outlined above. This can be promoted by addressing the intriguing knowledge relations to follow. They form part of the previously sketched new culture of knowledge. Each of these relationships can and should be impregnated by this new culture of knowledge. All of them are terms with which we are familiar and terms that form part of inflationary abusive knowledge strategies, but these terms should be reinvented, rearticulated and newly understood in terms of the new knowledge culture. This obligation, 'our absolute moral duty to pursue knowledge to the greatest possible degree', rests squarely on the shoulders of all knowledge workers in all sectors of society. See Michel Serres (1997) on the theme of 'the troubadour of knowledge' for a well-articulated description of the contemporary knowledge worker. I believe the five themes of complexity, understanding, intelligence, thinking and communication are of decisive importance in this respect if we wish to move forward in our 'knowledge' society in a significant way.

### 7.5.1   Knowledge and complexity

The notion of complexity needs careful attention since it is the only notion that can possibly safeguard us against the pitfalls of simplicity and oversimplification which are severe and even fatal since they are a distortion of reality. Bachelard (1985: 4) emphasises: 'The simple is always the simplified' and as such a distortion. The complex is not something from which to run. It is our biggest challenge, our ultimate test. We simply have to explore, grasp and articulate it. To hide away from it, especially behind the simple and the accessible, means to miss everything. Humans are not simple; reality is not accessible; the world is not given — no matter what we are willing to say about them.

We expect human thinking to dissipate obscurities and bring clarity and order to the real. The word 'complexity' can somehow only express our embarrassment and confusion, our incapacity to define in any simple way, to name in a clear fashion and to bring order to our ideas. Complexity is a problematic word and not a word of solution. Morin (1990) offers us an excellent introduction into the notion of complexity. Complexity is not so much the key to the world as a challenge posed by the world. Complex thinking is not a matter of avoiding or suppressing this challenge by way of relieving it and even overcoming it by properly articulating it and then linking it to the notion of meaning.

Because the complex will never fade away or disappear and because the experience of the full wealth of reality depends on it, the quest for understanding becomes urgent.

### 7.5.2 Knowledge, understanding and value

Unfortunately we cannot simply ignore the intimate link between knowledge and *understanding* (cf. Stiegler, 2010: 110). People may know a lot without understanding what they know, but is that really knowledge? Only knowledge which is properly understood has *value*. We all know how important values are in human life. And values bring *meaning* to a human situation. At this juncture can we really start talking about information, its usefulness and its meaning?

Understanding presupposes grasping the core issues, the totality and the general on which Laszlo (1989) is very explicit. The term 'world' fulfils a specific function here and is of crucial significance. For example, the struggle over the existence of the world, which was a major issue during the first half of the twentieth century, is at the same time, a struggle over our own existence. The globalisation debate and related matters are indeed worldly issues and call for thorough understanding as part of the effort to understand the present.

The ability to know through understanding depends on another human quality, the quality of intelligence.

### 7.5.3 Knowledge and intelligence

For knowledge to come to full fruition human intelligence must be fully explored and reinvented. We know and accept the fact that knowledge and the infinite verb 'to know' are related to intelligence, human intelligence in particular, rather than to machine or artificial intelligence. When we want to distinguish between these two intelligences the following is crucial: human intelligence rests on the substratum of living bodies while machine intelligence has no living body and may as such not even be referred to as intelligence in the true sense of the word. Knowledge in the true sense requires that we talk intelligently about what we know, not unintelligently or simply because it is fashionable.

Intelligence means literally 'to read between (the lines)', to find and establish connections between lines, but also between ideas, between different intelligences and even between people.

What is quite remarkable at present is that we cling to a very one-sided and superficial notion of knowledge to which I would like to refer to as, or link to, sentimental intelligence. Sentimental intelligence refers to a one-sided and very superficial notion of intelligence built on sentiments which are fairly unfounded, but with an appeal to all sorts of loyalties, preferences and prejudices: race, country, family, politics, ideologies, religious convictions and others. This intelligence type totally ignores the notion of complexity.

We have to distinguish between various other intelligences as well which we have to relate to knowledge: emotional, economic and rational. They are all important but need to be linked. As a matter of fact, how far can we really get with any one of these modes of intelligence on their own? Is this not the reason why there is no real progress in, for instance, education, upliftment and development? Words and things are not only directly linked but also operate, are functional, in a closely knit cooperation.

Humans have the capacity to accommodate the different levels of intelligence and move between them in a significant way. This capacity is the capacity to think and to think compositionally in anticipation of section 7.6.

### 7.5.4  Knowledge and thinking

Knowledge and intelligence are not indifferent to another superb and unique human quality, namely thinking, but thinking not in the abused sense of embracing the dogmatic, but thinking as an involvement with and commitment to values and inspired by and emerging from values (cf. Deleuze, 1983: 103−5).

Here I wish to introduce the Greek term *nous* as human thoughtfulness that describes thinking in an excellent way, but which is the neglected dimension here and should be reinvented since the Romans decided to leave it untranslated so it never became part of our vocabulary (Dreyfus & Dreyfus, 1988). Edgar Morin (1991) links the life and organisation of ideas − the food of thinking − in a thorough manner to what he calls the *noosphere* (Morin, 1991:105−56) and *noology* (Morin, 1991: 161−209) respectively. The noetic capacity does the linking, the noetic being the integrating partner. It links together the different levels of intelligence and integrates them into collective intelligence. The acceptance of collective intelligence brings about intelligent communities in which the new knowledge culture can flourish.

In the last analysis we cannot avoid attending to the noetic as human thoughtfulness in the fullest and richest sense, which we have at the same time to relate to the notion of wisdom, while wisdom forces us to relate to values − values not merely as an economic or market term as has become standard today, but values in a much wider sense. When I buy a painting for R5,000, the monetary value of the painting is only one aspect of its value. The value of its meaning to me cannot be calculated in monetary terms. It has a specific aesthetic value for me with an impact on my mental state and my emotional experiences. Have you ever seen the sublime expression on a human face after absorbing the beauty of a painting or a flower — the transforming power of the aesthetic, of plain beauty, is at issue here. Wisdom relates the knowable, the valuable and the beautiful and when combined they generate meaning.

### 7.5.5  Knowledge and communication or knowledge networks (the atlas of knowledges)

Serres (1969) uses two terms in this context, namely *linearity* or *the straight line* (Shannon) and tabularity or the network. Not dialogue, which is generally proposed as a solution, but plural speech or infinite conversation is emphasised by Blanchot (1993: 80—2). Dialogue is based on equality and sameness and therefore cannot work because there is no equality in societies. He proposes plural speech which is based on difference and seeks to receive the other as other and the foreign as foreign in their irreducible strangeness. We have to stop thinking only with a view to sameness and hence to unity. We should not fear to affirm interruption and rupture in order to express a truly plural speech — dissuading rather than persuading. This is the only speech which can accommodate the new knowledge culture.

The theory and practice of knowledge networks need proper elaboration. For an excellent recent exploration of the network idea see *Penser les reseaux* (*Thinking the Networks*) (Parrochia, 2001). The idea of network is currently particularly fashionable. Everyone wants to see it and have it installed everywhere. Beyond the fashionable, the utopian and the dreamlike there are several very valuable reasons for this involvement with networks, many of them developed and spelled out in this book. The contributions of cell phones and the Internet are no minor contributions in this field. In fact it seems as if humans have at last become what, in essence, they are: thinking networks. In this regard the contribution of Castells (1997) on 'the rise of the network society' and the way in which networks characterise contemporary societies and institutions is valuable.

Perhaps we need to consider the notion of 'new knowledge' here. It is equally necessary to consider the idea of knowledge networks, or the atlas of knowledges, sharing knowledges and acknowledging knowledges by which new knowledge emerges. Authentic knowledge is not necessarily the quality belonging to my view of knowledge. That is the reason why sharing and conversation become issues. We have to come to terms with knowledge in real terms, not in terms of sentiments, economics, emotions or reason, but in a comprehensive sense, under the guidance of our noetic or noologic capacities. This demanding issue requires full-time and diligent attention, but it is as rewarding as it is demanding. It brings excitement, light, the ability to distinguish and vision.

## 7.6  Language, intellectual capabilities and the use of terminology (vocabulary building)

In order to accommodate the idea of an atlas of knowledges and what it entails the reinvention and reorganisation of terminological issues related to the knowing of

**Table 7.1 Descriptive terms reflecting diverse perspectives on knowledge of the real**

| Representation | Dissemination (Derrida) |
|---|---|
| Continuity | Discontinuity (Nancy) |
| Grammar | Rhetoric (Lacan) |
| Rule | Paradox (Lyotard) |
| Linearity | Tabularity (Serres) |
| Tree | Rhizome (Deleuze) |
| Homogeneity | Heterogeneity (Serres) |
| Crystal | Smoke (Atlan) |
| Necessity | Chance (Monod) |
| Calculation | Unpredictability (Ekeland) |

**Table 7.2 Plurality of thinking dispositions**

| L'esprit de finesse | L'esprit de géometrie (Pascal) |
|---|---|
| Meditation | Representation (Heidegger) |
| Wisdom | Intelligence (Weizenbaum) |
| Judgement | Calculation (Wiezenbaum) |
| Speculative intellect | Aggressive intellect (Jonas) |
| Aesthetics | Calculus (Wersig) |
| Reason | Intelligence (Fromm) |

the real (Table 7.1) and to the thinking of and about the real (Table 7.2) are required. New knowledge and vocabulary building are intimately related. Different terms open different perspectives. This is the only way to deal with the new knowledge culture as expressed in the idea of an atlas of knowledges and knowledge networks. Words and language are crucial in the effort to articulate the developments to which we refer. Granger stated the situation superbly:

> *Science is a discourse; he who passes over this condition in silence runs a great risk of losing his way completely. In fact if this aspect of science is ignored, nothing is left but a bundle of techniques, or more precisely, some series of badly connected gestures, effective perhaps, but static, proposing nothing to the mind but an exact and servile initiation, bearing in themselves no force of expansion and progress ... [F]or scientific knowledge language is not only a vehicle between different minds, but also a mediator between one mind and its objects. (1983: 13)*

Consider, for example, the powerful role of the term *representation*. In its growth to power it hides the importance of many other terms which will expand our horizons and also our understanding of knowledge. Representation reflects, for instance, a realistic epistemology which conceives of representation as the reproduction, for subjectivity, of objectivity that lies outside it. It projects a mirror theory of knowledge and art (cf. Rorty's *Philosophy and the Mirror of Nature* (1982)), whose fundamental evaluative categories are those of adequacy, accuracy and truth itself. Not only is our scientific work hampered by this focus, but also our dealings with people in all sorts of situations — family, education, management, politics, therapy, religious convictions, medicine and many more. For this reason we refer to 'the curse of representation'. (See also the remark by Michel Serres (1989a: 97) along these lines when he refers to 'the drug of representation'.) For examples of other terms from the literature see Table 7.1.

Each term sketches a world in its own right and reinforces, amplifies and elaborates on this term. An example is perhaps the word 'dissemination'. Knowledge dissemination can refer to the distribution or sowing of seeds, which includes the promise of growth, a new birth, invention. If representation is close to repetition then dissemination is the expression of newness. Repetition spells stagnation; newness refers to new beginnings. True knowledge carries in itself the possibility of its own continuous renewal. But then it must be true knowledge. The domain of new knowledge is a domain of abundance and not of need, a domain of irreduction and not of reduction.

A specific view of thought corresponds to this notion of representation, best articulated by Heidegger in his distinction between representative or calculative thinking and contemplative or meditative thinking. Do not forget that thinking and knowing go hand in hand. Compare a number of additional terms used in the literature to widen the scope and expand the meaning of our understanding of thinking. One has already been mentioned, namely 'meditation' or 'meditative thought'. Although this term can be used in religious contexts it can also operate independently from religious activities. It can simply mean to go beyond the positive, the material and sense perception by which new domains are opening up. See Table 7.2 for more examples of 'diverse forms of thinking which designate the diverse moments, articulations and the multiple dimensions of the fact of knowledge' (Levinas, 1984: 12). The ultimate would be to view these terms, not as binary oppositions, but as complementary activities of thought that ultimately culminate in what can be called compositional thinking where they are all in some way interrelated as well as integrated.

## 7.7 Conclusion

Complexity, understanding, collective intelligence, thinking and communication networks are universal human phenomena which especially in their reinvented sense — quality and status — are of global importance. All talk about globalisation without attending to these issues will be in vain and counterproductive.

Any effort to understand the current conception and status of knowledge, linked to the above, requires us to understand it in relation to *globalisation* which of course also implies a link with information and communication technologies. We can no longer afford to remain fixed to the local. Knowledge networks in cyberspace involve every one of us as well as our countries. There is a lot of talk about the digital divide and the possibilities of narrowing the gap. This narrowing requires devotion, inputs, effort and discipline. We cannot block progress in order to catch up. Nobody will wait for us. We simply have to learn to run faster.

> *The prosperity of a nation, geographical region, business or individual, depends on the ability to navigate the knowledge space and explore the rich, new knowledge culture in its full complexity. Power is now conferred through the optimal management of knowledge, whether it involves technology, science, communication, or our ethical relationship with the other. The more we are able to form intelligent communities, as open-minded, cognitive, thoughtful subjects capable of initiative, imagination, inventiveness and rapid response to challenges, the more we will be able to ensure our success in a highly competitive globalised environment. In the long term, everything is based on the flexibility and vitality of our networks of knowledge production, transaction and exchange and a comprehensive understanding of the dynamics of all aspects of and stakeholders in these knowledge processes.*
>
> *(Lévy, 1997: 1)*

# References

Alavi, M., & Leidner, D. E. (2001). Knowledge management and knowledge management systems: Conceptual foundations and research issues. *MIS Quarterly, 25*(1), 107–136.

Assad, M. L. (1999). *Reading with michel serres: An encounter with time.* New York: SUNY Press.

Authier, M., & Lévy, P. (1996). *Les arbres de connaissances.* Paris: La Découverte.

Bachelard, G. (1985). *The new scientific spirit.* New York: Beacon Press.

Barrau, A., & Nancy, J.-L. (2011). *Dans quel monde vivons-nous?* Paris: Galilée.

Bernardis, M.-A., & Hagene, B. (1995). *Mesures et démesures.* Paris: La Cité des Sciences et de l'Industrie.

Blanchot, M. (1993). *The infinite conversation.* Minneapolis, MN: University of Minnesota Press.

Breton, P. (2000). *Le culte de l'internet: Une menace pour le lien social?* Paris: La Découverte.

Castells, M. (1997). *The rise of the network society.* Oxford: Blackwell.

Colebrook, C. (2000). Questioning representation. *SubStance, 29*(2), 47–67.

Deleuze, G. (1983). *Nietzsche and philosophy.* London: Athlone Press.

Dreyfus, H., & Dreyfus, S. (1988). *Mind over machine.* New York: Free Press.

Felman, S. (1987). *Jacques lacan and the adventure of insight: Psychoanalysis in contemporary culture.* Cambridge, MA: Harvard University Press.

Gadamer, H.-G. (1975). *Truth and method.* London: Sheed & Ward.

Gadamer, H.-G. (1996). *The enigma of health: The art of healing in a scientific age.* Cambridge: Polity Press.

Graham, G. (1999). *The internet: A philosophical inquiry.* London: Routledge.

Granger, G.-G. (1983). *Language as a vehicle of information. Formal thought and the sciences of man.* Dordrecht: D. Reidel.

Gray, CH. (Ed.), (1995). *The cyborg handbook* New York: Routledge.

Guattari, F. (1995). *Chaosmosis: An ethico-aesthetic paradigm.* Bloomington, IN: Indiana University Press.

Haraway, D. J. (1991). *Simians, cyborgs, and women: The reinvention of nature.* London: Free Association Books.

Hayles, N. K. (1999). *How we became posthuman: Virtual bodies in cybernetics, literature, and informatics*. Chicago: University of Chicago Press.

Heidegger, M. (1968). *What is called thinking?* New York: Harper & Row.

Hillis, K. (1999). *Digital sensations: Space, identity and embodiment in reality*. Minneapolis, MN: University of Minnesota Press.

Ihde, D. (2002). *Bodies in technology*. Minneapolis, MN: University of Minnesota Press.

Illich, I. (1973). *Tools for conviviality*. London: Calder & Boyars.

Johnstone, J. (1998). *Information multiplicity: American fiction in the age of media saturation*. Baltimore, MD: Johns Hopkins University Press.

Kristeva, J. (1980). *Desire in language: A semiotic approach to literature and art*. New York: Columbia University Press.

Kurzweil, R. (2000). *The age of the spiritual machine: When computers exceed human intelligence*. New York: Penguin Putnam.

Laszlo, E. (1989). *The inner limits of mankind: Heretical reflections on today's values, culture and politics*. London: One World Publications.

Latour, B. (1996). *Aramis, or the love of technology*. Cambridge, MA: Harvard University Press.

Levinas, E. (1984). *Transcendance et intelligibilité*. Geneva: Labor et Fides.

Levinas, E. (1985). *Ethics and infinity*. Pittsburgh: Duquesne University Press.

Lévy, P. (1993). *Les technologies de l'intelligence: l'avenir de la pensée à l' ère informatique*. Paris: Seuil (Points).

Lévy, P. (1997). *Collective intelligence: Mankind's emerging world in cyberspace*. New York: Plenum Trade.

Lévy, P. (1998). *Becoming virtual: Reality in the digital age*. New York: Plenum Trade.

Lévy, P. (2001). *Cyberculture*. Minneapolis, MN: University of Minnesota Press.

Lyotard, J.-F. (1988). *Peregrinations: Law, form, event*. New York: Columbia University Press.

Mandelbrot, B. B. (1982). *The Fractal Geometry of Nature*. San Francisco: Freeman.

Morin, E. (1990). *Introduction à la pensée complexe*. Paris: ESF éditeur.

Morin, E. (1991). *La Méthode 4: Les idées: leur habitat, leur vie, leurs mœurs, leur organisation*. Paris: Seuil.

Morin, E. (2001). *La Méthode 5: L'Humanité de l'humanité: l'identité humaine*. Paris: Seuil.

Myerson, G. (2001). *Heidegger, habermas and the mobile phone*. Reading: Cox Budrich.

Nancy, J.-L. (1997). *The sense of the world*. Minneapolis, MN: University of Minnesota Press.

Nancy, J.-L. (2000). *Corpus*. Paris: Éditions Metailié.

Nancy, J.-L. (2007). *The creation of the world or globilisation*. Albany, NY: SUNY Press.

Nelson, T. (1980). *Literary machines*. Sausalito, CA: Mindful Press.

Parrochia, D. (2001). *Penser les reseaux*. Seyssel: Éditions Champ Vallon.

Paulson, W. R. (1988). *The noise of culture: Literary texts in a world of information*. Ithaca, NY: Cornell University Press.

Peitgen, H. O., & Richter, P. H. (1986). *The beauty of fractals*. Berlin: Springer Verlag.

Poster, M. (2001). *What's the matter with the internet?* Minneapolis, MN: University of Minnesota Press.

Ronell, A. (1989). *The telephone book: Technology, schizophrenia, electric speech*. Lincoln, NB: University of Nebraska Press.

Rorty, R. (1982). *Philosophy and the mirror of nature*. Princeton, NJ: Princeton University Press.

Rutsky, R. L. (1999). *High techne: Art and technology from the machine aesthetic to the posthuman*. Minneapolis, MN: University of Minnesota Press.

Serres, M. (1969). *Hermès I: La communication*. Paris: Minuit.

Serres, M. (1972). *Hermès II: L'Interference*. Paris: Minuit.

Serres, M. (1975). *Feux et le signaux de brume: Zola*. Paris: Grasset.

Serres, M. (1980). *Hermès V: Passage du Nord-Ouest*. Paris: Minuit.

Serres, M. (1987a). *Statues*. Paris: François Bourin.

Serres, M. (1987b). *L'Hermaphrodite: Sarrasine sculpteur*. Paris: Flammarion.

Serres, M. (1989a). *Detachment*. Athens, OH: Ohio University Press.

Serres, M. (1989b). Literature and the exact sciences. *SubStance*, *18*(2), 3–34.

Serres, M. (Ed.), (1989c). *Elements d'Histoire des sciences* Paris: Bordas.

Serres, M. (1993). *Les origines de la géometrie*. Paris: Flammarion.

Serres, M. (1994a). *Atlas*. Paris: Julliard.

Serres, M. (1994b). *Angels: A modern myth*. Paris: Flammarion.

Serres, M. (1995a). *Genesis*. Ann Arbor, MI: University of Michigan Press.

Serres, M. (1995b). *Conversations on science, culture, and time* (with Bruno Latour). Ann Arbor, MI: University of Michigan Press.

Serres, M. (1995c). *The natural contract*. Ann Arbor, MI: University of Michigan Press.

Serres, M. (1997). *The troubadour of knowledge*. Ann Arbor, MI: University of Michigan Press.

Serres, M. (1999). *Variations sur le corps*. Paris: Le Pommier-Fayard.

Serres, M. (2001). *Hominescence*. Paris: le Pommier.

Serres, M. (2007). *The parasite*. Minneapolis, MN: University of Minnesota Press.

Serres, M. (2014). *Pantomie: de Hermès à petite poucette*. Paris: Le Pommier.

Shapiro, M. J. (1999). *Moral spaces: Rethinking ethics and world politics*. Minneapolis, MN: University of Minnesota Press.

Spinner, H. (1994). *Die Wissensordnung: Ein Leitkonzept für die dritte Grundordnung des Informationszeitalters*. Opladen: Leske & Budrich.

Stiegler, B. (1994). *La technique et le temps: 1. La faute d'Epimethée*. Paris: Galilée.

Stiegler, B. (1996). *La technique et le temps: 2. La désorientation*. Paris: Galilée.

Stiegler, B. (2001). *La technique et le temps: 3. Le temps du cinéma et la question du mal-être*. Paris: Galilée.

Stiegler, B. (2010). *Taking care of youth and the generations*. Stanford, CA: Stanford University Press.

Stiegler, B. *La technique et le temps: 4. Symboles et diaboles ou la guerre des esprits*. Paris: Galilée (forthcoming).

Stiegler, B. *La technique et le temps: 5. Le defaut qu'il faut*. Paris: Galilée (forthcoming).

Stiegler, B., & Ars Industrialis (2006). *Réenchanter le monde: la valeur esprit contre le populisme industriel*. Paris: Flammarion.

SubStance (1993) Epistemocritique, 22 (2/3) (Special Issue).

Virilio, P. (2001). *Cybermonde, la politique du pire*. Paris: Les Editions Textuel.

# The contemporary knowledge worker (the troubadour of knowledge): comprehensive and exciting challenges

**8**

## 8.1 Introduction: the new knowledge age and its challenges

The knowledge worker is a central or key figure in knowledge organisation. It was always the case and will always be the case. There cannot be knowledge organisation without a knowledge organiser, in other words the involvement of human beings in the informatisation processes. Although this is a truism it is not, for some reason, the main focus of our interest, although this should be the case (see Wersig, 1993; Wiig, 2004). Currently, however, this figure becomes even more important in view of the new dispensation of knowledge where knowledge becomes the characterising factor of our age, where theoretical developments regarding knowledge and its nature force us in the direction of what can be called 'a new knowledge dispensation' (De Beer, 2009; also De Beer, 2007). What exactly is new in this new dispensation?

The new knowledge dispensation refers to dramatic contemporary changes in the knowledge-world that relate to a number of things. In the *first* place it is a world in which, different from before, inter-disciplinarity, multi-disciplinarity and trans-disciplinarity become such defining notions of knowledge activities in our age that it cannot be ignored. In this way the scientific landscape has been changed in a significant way. Knowledge workers are compelled to attend to it. *Secondly*, knowledge networks under the comprehensive impact of information and communication technologies are such influential resources, altogether different from before. This changes the character, not only of knowledge, but also of our approach to the authority of knowledges. In the *third* place, a new culture has been established, called cyberculture by Lévy (2001) and others. The core of this newly established culture is knowledge, and new contexts for knowledge development and the understanding of knowledge have been created in the process. This knowledge culture becomes a central issue in societies which knowledge workers have to reckon with. In the *fourth* place, the impact of these technical developments on our understanding of humans is immense. A new image of the human person is in the process of taking shape. The notion of the so-called 'post-human' emerged. Fukuyama (2003) and Lecourt (2003), to mention only two, have made significant contributions in this regard. We can and

Information Science as an Interscience.

should expect an equally immense impact on the knowledge organiser. I miss this emphasis on what it means to be human in the literature on knowledge organisation. In *fifth* place, the implication of these dramatic developments inspires a dramatic impact on inter-human relations and societal dynamics. For this reason there is currently an intense search for a new conceptualisation of our understanding of human society and a quest for new foundations, focusing on the notion of the 'us' that has been or has got lost in recent times. Certainly a new kind of society and community is the issue here. What, for instance, is the implication for knowledge workers and knowledge organisation when the notion of a knowledge society emerges so strongly? If a knowledge society is to be established and allowed to flourish, human individuals who are knowledgeable about the issues mentioned should at least come forward willing to accept the comprehensive, but also exciting, challenges.

These developments during the past few decades, taken together, have had drastic consequences for all facets of knowledge work and activities. They put enormous pressure on and pose fascinating challenges to all activities related to knowledge organisation. From such a perspective it becomes an imperative to take a close look at and rethink this key figure of the knowledge worker, with the understanding that no knowledge organisation can materialise without the knowledge worker. As has been stated already, there cannot be any knowledge organisation without knowledge organisers. And the qualities required from such a figure that will enable this person, or such persons, to make significant contributions in this context and domain of activity are fascinating.

As the point of departure I wish to posit the notion of the 'troubadour of knowledge' (borrowed from Michel Serres, 1997), or the configurer of knowledge, as the most adequate name for the anticipated new characterisation of the figure of the knowledge worker, knowledge organiser or information professional. The intention is to sketch this figure as that most needed for our turbulent times − turbulent both with regard to socio-cultural, economic and political issues and to the burning issues of knowledge sketched above. This figure reflects Michel Serres' identification of the figure of the troubadour with the instructed third (see Section 8.2) and his or her equation of learning and knowing with finding and inventing (Serres, 1989, 1995, 1997). The troubadour refers to the poet-musicians who travelled through medieval Provence (in France), collecting material from all kinds of sources for the eventual enriching entertainment of communities through their performances. Throughout his study Serres emphasises that knowledge, learning and philosophy are linked to travel, to seeking, to encountering, to the intersection of genres and of disciplines, and to the felicitous use of language. But what can such a person use to do just this, to comply with these requirements? The answer includes insight, in terms of understanding the audience and its needs, as well as an understanding of knowledges and instruments, especially given the range of instruments currently available!

The troubadour can do precisely this because this figure is a progressive learner and learns everything; does not specialise or does not only specialise; does not learn only what falls within the academic ambit; the eternal learner who learns everywhere; and then the configurer, the facilitator who can and wants to bring to life every kind of knowledge at every place and time and make it available for a wider range of contexts and needs. This person is in fact a key figure — every organisation needs at least one of them. The information and knowledge profession needs many of them — all of its workers should be such figures. People need to be educated for this. Every institution and organisation that has realised the value of such a figure has begun in some cases or should begin as soon as possible to ensure its future. Higher education, in order to make significant contributions, should consider the cultivation of 'the instructed third' in every teacher, educator, scientist as its ultimate objective.

Not only Michel Serres (1989, 1995, 1997), but also Davenport (1999, 2005), Gibbons (2000), Gibbons et al. (1994), Nowotny, Scott, and Gibbons (2004), Wiig (1993), Wersig (1990) and Kuhlen (2004), from our own field, have alluded to some of these ideas in an exciting way, indicating to what extent the dynamic nature of knowledges and the sciences and the special figure of the knowledge worker are intricately related, or should deliberately and methodically be related. A new and vast field has been opened up due to the rethinking of the sciences, including the information sciences. This new field poses enormous challenges to people involved in all areas of knowledge work and the development of a knowledge culture.

What are the special requirements for the knowledge worker, the knowledge organiser, the troubadour of knowledge, given the above characterisation of the contemporary era?

1. They should develop sensitivity towards knowledges, all knowledges — the instructed third.
2. They should be willing to navigate, travel, search in a special mode that complies with the new knowledge dispensation.
3. There must be a keenness to become an eternal learner — who never stops but is always looking for new knowledge and insight.
4. An equally eager enthusiasm to read and to read well, but to read differently, will be an essential requirement.
5. The overwhelming challenge of the contemporary situation is to excel in thinking, to refuse to merely repeat what is given or to fall into the trap of repetitive thinking.
6. A commitment to engage in an 'eternal conversation' with a willingness to cross boundaries is non-negotiable.
7. All these qualities will emerge from a well-developed imaginative noetic capacity as its condition — human beings are spiritual beings and this quality should be manifested in their enthusiasm.
8. Inevitably this will lead to inventiveness for real problem-solving in a new way, which is not fake.

## 8.2  An exploration of the new qualities of the knowledge worker to be reinvented

1. This person is called 'the instructed third', is competent and is most capable of linking the sciences (the instructed first) with the humanities (the instructed second), while taking him/herself the third position, that is the position between the two, with the ability to move from one to the other and back again — a kind of traveller or voyager, hence the

troubadour. The 'instructed third' is the person who knows how to weave together the truth of the sciences with the peace of judgement; she/he is able to blend cultural heritages and legacies of knowledge since she/he is deeply rooted in both. Such a person is an expert in formal or experimental knowledge, is well-versed in the natural sciences of the inanimate and the living, is at a safe remove from the social sciences with their critical rather than organic truths and their banal, commonplace information, prefers actions to relations and direct human experience to surveys and documents, and is a traveller through nature and society. The instructed third facilitates communication between scientific knowledge and the humanities, is archaic and contemporary, traditional and futuristic, further removed from power than anybody else and closer to ignorance of the multitude, and knows well how to encourage invention, which is thinking rather than reproduction and repetition (see Serres, 1989, 1995 and 1997).

One thing seems to be clear: whoever wants to work in the knowledge field, whether it is called knowledge organisation, knowledge retrieval or information behaviour, needs to honour the interdisciplinary nature of this engagement that is emphasised in almost every relevant source in our field (see Authier & Lévy, 1996).

2. The troubadour needs to be a *traveller*, a voyager, a navigator who needs space, the space of knowledge, which is currently no longer a mere physical space, but a virtual space, also referred to as cyberspace (see Lévy, 1998). That this is part of our field is self-explanatory. Knowledge networks, due to computer networks, are creating this space to be navigated. The navigation activities have been used in knowledge and information work circles for some time now where knowledge networks are relevant. Navigating computer networks for new knowledge is not new in the contemporary field of information and knowledge work and is extremely important, especially because we have entered into a new knowledge dispensation for quite some time now. In this dispensation the local and the global must be linked. What is required is people able to move around in this space and comprehensively navigate it, to not be afraid of disciplinary boundaries but be fully aware of the value of all disciplines, and then collect whatever may be relevant from whatever source and configure these findings into meaningful knowledge entities that can make a difference to situations.

3. In order to qualify in the above sense the troubadour is, or should be, an eternal *learner* – uninhibited and with never-ending devotion. The portrait of the instructed third is informed by a learning process resembling a voyage, motion, bifurcations, becoming and changes. Being a learner means becoming manifold, developing a capacity for all meanings in diverse directions, being a human person on its way to adulthood of thought and invention. In the business world the notion of learning organisations certainly also involves individuals in the organisations and is not new but is of high importance (see Argyris, 1993, 1998; Ellis, 1988). Libraries are in a unique way learning organisations of sorts. This is a special requirement for knowledge workers should they want to cope with challenges related to this culture of the learning organisation. Wenger (1998), in his emphasis on communities of practice, has chosen as a subtitle: learning, meaning and identity. Note the emphasis on 'community'.

4. In order to learn properly and to the maximum the troubadour will be and should be a *reader*, not in the generally accepted sense only, but in a very special sense: reading dynamically with non-linear concepts, focusing on the dynamic quality of texts as a whole which may be called non-linear, and with a careful reflection on all the above-mentioned issues. The reader is therefore well-advised not to concentrate on preferred fragments only since she/he will then miss the inventive creativity of the multiple whole and thus fall short of an unpredictable but complete understanding of poetic beauty and inventive imagination. In this regard understanding is of the utmost importance, understanding of users and their needs and of knowledges. If knowledge workers want to deliver a sensible

service to clients they certainly have to be adequately informed about diverse aspects of knowledge and information and understand the dynamics of these notions well. Reading is one ability that will enable them to perform well in this regard. There are many modes of reading and one special feature in this context is the work done on rhizomatic reading by Burnett (2002), a colleague in our field. What is self-evident is a sensitivity towards matters of language as something much more than a mere tool (see De Beer, 2014).

5. Moving around through learning and reading stimulates another uniquely human ability, namely *thinking*, but again a special kind of thinking: we must make a qualitative leap to and into a new way of thinking. We have to appreciate the fact that being exposed to a virtual knowledge reality with global dimensions and implications, in addition to a different scientific dynamic, will most certainly expect or insist on a new kind or mode of thinking adequate to articulate what we encounter.

Thinking must here be understood not in the traditionally accepted sense of representation and repetition alone, but in the sense of freedom of movement, of transgressing boundaries, of linking the unlinkable, of leaving the marked roads and moving into the unexpected and the unpredictable.

Our normal understanding of thinking does not create room for a thinking that can deal with the virtual, while this is exactly what is required from this new mode of thinking. Virtuality does not refer to some false or imaginary world. On the contrary it is the very dynamic of a shared world; it is that through which we share reality. A thought, multiple in nature and activity, that accommodates virtuality will be able to discover and explore new forms of truth that accompany the dynamic of virtualisation (see Lévy, 1998: 183–7). In this way opportunities will be opening up for inventions.

In the related field of knowledge management, the knowledge worker has been described as a thinker in the sense of making a living through thinking (Davenport, 2005). In view of the systematic efforts of the killing of thinking as has been highlighted by Evans (2004), we have to repossess our ability to think at all costs. For Wiig (1993) 'thinking about thinking' constitutes the foundations for knowledge management. For these reasons knowledge workers should cultivate their capacity to think.

6. All these qualities are communal qualities and do not find expression in a solipsistic way or sense and for this reason the quality of *infinite conversation* (Blanchot, 1993) should be added. No knowledge worker can proceed without conversation of a kind. Quality of conversation is required and Blanchot proposes conversation rather than dialogue because it means literally 'to turn to one another' and to move forward together despite differences. Von Krogh, Ichijo, and Nonaka (2000) add their voices to this idea with the emphasis on 'managing conversations' – conversations as care-full activities and initiatives (see also Von Krogh, 1998). These ideas are immensely reinforced by the emphasis on 'community in the context of knowledge work (Davenport & Hall, 2002; Lévy, 1997; Wenger, 1998).

7. These six characteristics of the knowledge worker (the troubadour) converge in *the imaginative noetic capacity*, or, alternatively:

*These characteristics emerge from the cultivation of the noetic capacity, the supreme but currently neglected capacity of humans by which they are emitted in all directions in order to keep the human world moving, just like a prism which collects and emits by means of culture, science, technics, thought and action which are continuously subjected to the interactive autopoietic spiral of existence and the dynamic spiral of imagination in the process of establishing intelligent communities that calls for commitment, practice and justice.*

*(Lévy, 1997: 245–55)*

What this really means is that wisdom is required, guaranteed by the imaginative noetic capacity. For wisdom to materialise the embracement of this capacity is a condition and the only way to defeat the fatal neglect mentioned above. To honour our profession it would be wise also to embrace the work done in this regard by Melot (2004) in his articulation of 'the wisdom of the librarian'. In other words, this idea of the noetic imagination is not at all foreign to literature in our field. And let us never forget: the much-mentioned, but also highly questionable, information pyramid of data, information, knowledge, wisdom can never reach fulfilment unless knowledge workers act wisely.

8. The outcome of what has been discussed up till now takes us to what we need most: *invention* – the ultimate in human action. Soon after I became intrigued with the term invention, as if it is something new, thanks to Michel Serres' explicit remarks on it with his significant statement: 'I invent therefore I am', I discovered how many texts have already written about this theme. To name a few: invention is a social act (LeFevre, 1987), inventive humans (Bloom, 2002) and reinventing spirituality for our day and age (Stiegler & Ars Industrialis, 2006). Nor should it be forgotten that Hannah and Harris (1999), from the heart and core of the library and information sciences, wrote about inventiveness, especially the invention of the future.

## 8.3   Conclusion

The term invention, that is my suggestion, is the real focus of 'the instructed third' – the knowledge worker in the true sense of the word. Human knowledge is in any case about action. The above paragraphs on the qualities of the knowledge worker sketch the conditions for inventions on a grand scale, especially the inventions of new knowledges for special actions. Complying with these conditions will make the appearance of new things a natural happening. When inventiveness is combined with the dynamics of virtualisation, where the virtual is understood as 'a fecund and powerful mode of being that expands the process of creation, opens up the future, injects a core of meaning beneath the platitudes of immediate presence' (Lévy, 1998: 16), then new worlds, new futures, new human situations, new human dispositions and relations, a new sense of values, a new commitment to justice and new meaning in life will irrefutably emerge. But only if the spirit of invention is embraced and pursued in intelligent communities which at the same time are communities of commitment and communities of practice, and here it can be added: 'communities of justice'.

## References

Argyris, C. (1993). Education for leading-learning. *Organizational Dynamics, 21*(3), 5–17.
Argyris, C. (1998). *Teaching smart people how to learn. Harvard business review on knowledge management*. Harvard Business School Press.
Authier, M., & Lévy, P. (1996). *Les arbres de connaissances*. Paris: La Découverte.
Blanchot, M. (1993). *The infinite conversation*. Minneapolis, MN: University of Minnesota Press.

Bloom, H. (2002). *Genius: A mosaic of one hundred exemplary creative minds.* London: Fourth Estate.

Burnett, K. (2002). Rhizomatic reading: An ergodic literacy. *Encyclopedia of Library and Information Science, 72,* 315—341.

Davenport, E., & Hall, H. (2002). Organizational knowledge and communities of practice. In B. Cronin (Ed.), *Annual review of information science and technology* (Vol. 36). Medford, NJ: Information Today.

Davenport, T. H. (1999). *Saving IT's soul: Human centred information management. Harvard business review on the business value of IT.* Harvard Business School Press.

Davenport, T. H. (2005). *Thinking for a living: How to get better performance and results from knowledge workers.* Boston: Harvard Business School.

De Beer, C. S. (2007). Knowledge is everywhere: A philosophical exploration'. In B. R. Bravo, & L. A. Díez (Eds.), *Actas del VIII Congreso ISKO-España.* León: University of León Publications.

De Beer, C. S. (2009). Let the new knowledge come: Atlas of knowledges. In *IX congress ISKO-Spain: New perspectives for the organization and dissemination of knowledge,* Acta del Congreso, Vol. 1. Universitat Politécnica de Valencia (pp. 48—57).

De Beer, C. S. (2014). Reading: The understanding and invention of meaning. In J. S. Wessels, & J. C. Pauw (Eds.), *Reflective public administration: Context, knowledge and methods.* Pretoria: Unisa Press.

Ellis, J. (1988). Information management: Meaning and learning. *International Journal of Information Management, 8,* 35—42.

Evans, M. (2004). *Killing thinking: The death of the universities.* London: Continuum.

Fukuyama, F. (2003). *Our post-human future: Consequences of the biotechnology revolution.* New York: Picador.

Gibbons, M. (2000). What kind of university? Change of research practices. *Mousaion, 18* (1), 28—40.

Gibbons, M., Limoges, C., Nowotny, H., Schwartzmann, S., Scott, P., & Trow, M. (1994). *The new production of knowledge: The dynamics of science and research in contemporary societies.* London: Sage.

Hannah, S. A., & Harris, M. H. (1999). *Inventing the future: Information services for a new millennium.* Stamford: Ablex.

Kuhlen, R. (2004). *Informationsethik.* Konstanz: UVK Verlagsgesellschaft.

Lecourt, D. (2003). *Humain, posthumain.* Paris: PUF.

LeFevre, K. B. (1987). *Invention as a Social Act.* Carbonsdale, IL: Southern Illinois University Press.

Lévy, P. (1997). *Collective intelligence: Mankind's emerging world in cyberspace.* New York: Plenum Trade.

Lévy, P. (1998). *Becoming virtual: Reality in the digital age.* New York: Plenum Trade.

Lévy, P. (2001). *Cyberculture.* Minneapolis, MN: University of Minnesota Press.

Mason, R. O. (1990). What is an information professional? *Journal of Education for Library and Information Science, 31*(2), 122—138.

Melot, M. (2004). *La Sagesse du Bibliothécaire.* Paris: L'Oeil neuf éditions.

Nowotny, H., Scott, P., & Gibbons, M. (2004). *Re-thinking science: Knowledge and the public in the age of uncertainty.* Oxford: Polity Press.

Serres, M. (1989). Literature and the exact sciences. *SubStance, 18*(2), 3—34.

Serres, M. (1995). *Conversations on science, culture and time.* Ann Arbor, MI: University of Michigan Press.

Serres, M. (1997). *The troubadour of knowledge*. Ann Arbor, MI: University of Michigan Press.

Stiegler, B., & Ars Industrialis (2006). *Reenchanter le monde: La valeur esprit contre le populisme industriel*. Paris: Flammarion.

Von Krogh, G. (1998). Care in knowledge creation. *California Management Review, 40*(3), 133–153.

Von Krogh, G., Ichijo, K., & Nonaka, I. (2000). *Enabling knowledge creation: How to unlock the mystery of tacit knowledge and release the power of innovation*. Oxford: Oxford University Press.

Wenger, E. (1998). *Communities of practice: Learning, meaning, and identity*. New York: Cambridge University Press.

Wersig, G. (1990). The changing role of knowledge in an information society. In D. J. Foskett (Ed.), *The information environment: A world view* (pp. 190–197). New York: Elsevier Science.

Wersig, G. (1993). *Fokus Mensch: Bezugspunkte postmoderner Wissenschaft: Wissen, Kommunikation, Kultur*. Frankfurt am Main: Peter Lang.

Wiig, K. M. (1993). *Knowledge management foundations: Thinking about thinking*. Arlington, TX: Schema Press.

Wiig, K. M. (2004). *People-focused knowledge management*. Oxford: Elsevier.

# A proposed philosophico-ethical approach towards the electronic information era

**9**

## 9.1 Introduction

My point of departure is that there are, broadly speaking, two philosophical approaches: a critique philosophy and an acritical philosophy. This differentiation may also be important for information scientists to consider. Despite the major importance of practice in this domain, it should never be forgotten that all practices — educational practice, teaching practice, library practice, information practice, medical practice and all the other practices — are always informed by and as such determined by theory and philosophy. None of these practices can ever be separated from the ethics that should guide and direct them.

The differences between the two approaches mentioned are vast. The one has to do with controlling life and the other has to do with living life. The one understands thinking as manipulation; the other considers thinking as a way of life. The one considers ethics as something to be worked out, debated and organised in accordance with given or assumed rules; the other sees ethical issues as life, as living with others, with the world and with oneself. The one considers knowledge as manipulable entities; the other sees knowledge as dependent on life, the other, etc. The one thinks in order to do; the other considers thinking and doing as part of the same activity of living. The one refers to an eternal circular movement and the other to more of an upward spiral. The one innovates; the other invents. (See also Chapter 1.)

The essay by Bruno Latour (1987) on the philosophy of Michel Serres is of decisive inportance. His characterisation of Serres' philosophy as an 'acritical philosophy' is the guidance and inspiration for the focus of the present publication. The enlightening way in which he differentiates between the 'critique' tradition and the acritical approach will be relied on in the following pages. It is equally relevant for Chapter 1, as has already been indicated. It would be significant for and supportive of the argument to add the section from the Conversations between Latour and Serres on 'The End of Criticism' as well in which the same issues are re-emphasised quite strongly (see Serres, 1995: 125–66).

The implications of these different perspectives for information science and for information work in the information era are vast. These views and their implications will hopefully become clearer as the present chapter continues.

In order for us to grasp the idea of an acritical philosophy of information it is first of all required to come to terms clearly with the notions of a critical

Information Science as an Interscience.

philosophy and an acritical philosophy before we can get to an understanding of an acritical philosophy of information which is actually the core of our theme in terms of which a philosophico-ethical approach can be developed. It is important to emphasise that a critical approach generates an obstacle to the ethical while the acritical approach facilitates the ethical.

## 9.2   Assumptions of the 'critique' philosophers

Latour (1987: 85−92) characterises the philosophy of the 'critique' tradition as 'the discipline in charge of founding knowledge, debunking beliefs, adjudicating territories, ruling opinions'. And to this he adds:

> Critique philosophers firmly install their meta-language in the centre and slowly substitute their arguments to every single object of the periphery. Organizing the critique is tantamount to a careful, obstinate, empire building. A powerful critique, people say, is one that ties like a bicycle wheel every point of the periphery to one term of the centre through the intermediary of a proxy. At the end, holding the centre is tantamount to holding the world. A scholarly work is recognizable for the continuity, homogeneity and coherence of the metalanguage used all along to subsume periphery. (1987: 90)

Critique philosophers see their task as that of establishing a distinction between beliefs on the one hand and knowledge on the other, or between ideologies and science, or between democracy and terror, and others. Since Descartes we have been looking for the minimum that could be said to be safe and certain. We, the knights of the critique, do not ask much, provided we can hold to one thing, even minuscule: to the cogito, to the transcendent (and to move the world), to the class struggle, to language analysis, to discourse, to one tiny thing that allows us to see through the rest, and we will then feel happy and safe. The critique work is that of a reduction of the world into two packs: a little one that is sure and certain and the immense rest which is simply believed and in dire need of being criticised, founded, re-educated, straightened up. Out on rough water the critique always looks for a lifeboat (Latour, 1987: 85).

One has to choose between adjectives. We are sure! We distribute adjectives such as *outmoded, charming, poetic, rigorous, scientific, fictional, mythical* with great mastery. It is beyond doubt that there has been a Copernican revolution that started the Enlightenment and established science as the sure and definitive access to truth, away from religion and mythology. Science has outgrown its past and irreversibly passed over the Dark Ages of belief, opinion and storytelling. How can you doubt that? How can we deny this after Descartes, Comte and Bachelard (Latour, 1987: 84)? In this context it will make sense to study carefully the essay by Dupuy (2013) on 'science, a theology in spite of itself'.

Critique philosophers firmly install their metalanguage in the centre. The sad consequence is the unidentified link between this and objectivity, order and violence.

Science, critique, violence and order are not unrelated. The sciences were not a way to limit violence but to fuel it: 'Thanatocracy' (the power of death) Michel Serres (1972) calls it. That is why it is fair to state that the 'critique' tradition constitutes barriers and obstacles to the flourishing of the ethical. It can in this context only rely on powerless codes and rules. The mixing up of objectivity and violence is best visible in the ways in which scientific professions organise their trade. The critique tradition loves concepts and disciplines and hates whatever may be unwilling to comply. Order is the rule; disorder is what should be ignored at all cost.

The problem that imposes itself at this point relates to the fact that we who are working in the field of knowledge are so deeply entrenched in the securities of the system, of the metanarratives, of the conclusions and outcomes of our critical exercises, to say nothing about the final and definitive place and role allocated to 'library literacy, information literacy and computer literacy', that we are deeply unwilling to consider anything which poses a threat to these securities. We can hardly afford to consider alternatives. All these literacies will solve all our problems. As Dupuy (1980: 16) puts it: 'A new form of domination is appearing in which man is no longer dominated by man but in which men are managed by another anonymous collective entity: *mechanisms.*' Literacies are mechanical acquisitions which supposedly will overcome illiteracies easily. The problem is that these mechanisms do not know how to deal with differences, incommensurables, immeasurables and uncertainties. A whole part of whatever is, certainly the most significant part, consists of these aspects, issues and forces. We are trapped in a kind of simple-mindedness, while forgetting Bachelard's warning: the simple is always the simplified. And simplification is a form of reduction. To pretend that differences, incommensurables, immeasurables and uncertainties are not there and not real suggests that these pretenders are living in a fool's paradise. What is more serious, however, is the fact that extensive persuasive skills, mechanisms and tactics are nevertheless thoughtlessly applied to force everybody into this paradise, mostly exercised by technocrats, bureaucrats and economocrats. Paradisiacal or not: it is demonstrated by many that any assumption of final, absolute, perfect knowledge is precisely abolishing what we are hoping to achieve and that humans are desperately in need of: the emergence of new and renewed meaning.

Dretske (1981) and the debates about his work in the special issue of the philosophy journal *Synthese* shortly after the publication of his book are good examples of a critical approach related to information. Cognitivism, and its concerns about and applications to information and knowledge, are, of course, another prime example of the critique philosophy.

## 9.3   Towards an 'acritical' philosophy

Since that aspect of the real which is mostly consistently denied in both the theory and practice of the domains of technoscience, computer technology, telematics and the media is of such a decisive and such an absolutely significant nature, we have to reflect on it. We have to follow the suggestion of Bruno Latour (1988) with his 'irreductions', mentioned earlier in Chapters 2 and 4, which means: the protest against reductionism should be kept alive. This will be done in our context by emphasising some alternatives which should be considered, and which the philosophies of many noteworthy thinkers apart from Serres (Deleuze, Lyotard, Levinas) indeed imply. It should be fruitful to follow some of these leads in order to assess to what extent hopeful outcomes can be detected for further exploration. It will be important to pay attention to the core role of the ethical in all these cases.

### 9.3.1   The dogmatic and the new image of thought (Gilles Deleuze)

Deleuze (1983) distinguishes between two images of thought: the dogmatic and the new. Here we will literally follow the views expressed by Deleuze himself.

The dogmatic image of thought he summarised in three essential theses:

1. The thinker as thinker wants and loves truth; thought as thought possesses or formally contains truth; thinking is the natural exercise and it is therefore sufficient to think truly and to think with truth.
2. We are diverted from the truth by forces which are foreign to it (body, passions, sensuous interests). When we fall into error it is merely the effect, in thought as such, of external forces which are opposed to thought.
3. All we need to do is to think well, and in order to think well *what* we need, in a truthful way, is to have a method. Method brings us back to the nature of thought and through it we ward off the effect of the alien forces which alter it and distract us. It enables us to enter the domain of that which is valid for all times and places. (See Chapters 4 and 5 for reflections on method.)

These three theses constitute the essence of the 'critique' tradition as explored in Section 9.1.

According to this image of thought, truth is conceived of as an abstract universal. We are unfortunately, in this context, never referred to the real forces that form thought. Thought itself is never related to the real forces that it presupposes.

*But*, there is no truth that, before being a truth, is not the bringing into effect of a sense or meaning or *the* realisation of a value. Sense, or meaning, and value are the presuppositions of truth. Everything depends on the sense and value of what we think. We always have the truths we deserve as a function of the sense of what we conceive, of the value of what we believe. The truth of a thought must be interpreted and evaluated according to the forces or power that determine it to think, and to think this rather than that. We must always ask what forces are hiding themselves in the thought of this truth, and therefore what its sense and value is.

What the dogmatic image of thought conceals is the work of established forces and established powers that determine thought in its purity. The new image of thought means primarily that truth is not the element of thought. The element of thought is sense and value. The categories of thought are not truth and falsity but the noble and the base. Mature, considered thought has other enemies, negative states: stupidity and baseness. Stupidity expresses the non-sense in thought, its imbecility.

But it may be made up entirely of truths. These truths are base, they are those of a heavy soul. Stupidity, and more profoundly, that of which it is a symptom, a base way of thinking, is the expression of the state of mind dominated by reactive forces, by right. Stupid thought only discovers the most base: the reign of petty values, the power of an established order − the basis of the 'critique' tradition.

The new image of thought is thought which has as its most positive task the enterprise of demystification. Thinking renounces its role as demystifier when it gives up the harming of stupidity and the denunciation of baseness. This way of thinking is useful for turning stupidity into something shameful; its only use is the exposure of all forms of baseness of thought. This means that thought must be turned into something aggressive, active and affirmative which implies the creation of free humans who do not confuse the aims of cultivated humanity with the benefits of the state, moral philosophies or religion. The new image of thought suggests then the conquering of the negative and its false glamour. This represents an excellent description of the acritical disposition of thought.

The new image of thought is illustrated by Deleuze's development of notions like the *fold*, *vitality*, the *nomad* and the *multiple* which are all of particular importance in contemporary information science, the denial of which will be the ultimate in irresponsibility.

### 9.3.2 Homology and paralogy (Jean-François Lyotard)

One of the most significant and influential reflections yet on the information era and on the status of information in the contemporary world is offered by Lyotard (1984).

Two significant words used in this study are *homology* and *paralogy* − sameness and difference, simple and deep logic. It relates to the difference between knowledge and thinking as tools of authority, of the expert, of the metaphysician, the ideologist, of one who knows what he knows and does not know, on the one hand. In this case statements are made, critique applied and definitive conclusions reached. The 'critique' tradition is here well-defined. On the other hand, there is the knowledge of the comprehensive thinker. In this case thinking and knowledge refine our sensitivity to differences, and reinforce our ability to tolerate the incommensurable, but also to contemplate the sublime. This suits the acritical position perfectly. We are at the same time reminded of the fundamental place of agonistics which is particularly, in addition to the repsonsibility of comprehensiveness in thought and due to that among other things, a theme of ethical concern.

Homology is a clear exposition of the critique philosophy; paralogy is a demonstration of the acritical, of the multiple and nomadic, of the responsive. The above-mentioned notions of Deleuze clearly call for a paralogy rather than a homology.

The emphasis by both Deleuze's focus on values and Lyotard's on agonistics makes a consideration of the philosophical position of Levinas regarding the relationship between knowledge and ethics inevitable.

### 9.3.3 Ethics comes before knowledge (Levinas)

In Levinas' thinking the suggestions of Deleuze are taken to their ultimate consequences. In response to the question what it means to be alive in the world he insists on moral philosophy as the first philosophy which gives primacy to moral categories above all others. One can expect that he will pose the problem of knowledge and ethics from a totally different angle. He maintains, in opposition to the generally accepted view, that ethics is more fundamental and prior to knowledge. Knowledge makes sense only after the commitment of ethics. For Levinas, goodness comes first. (See for this paragraph the excellent exploration by Cohen (1986: 1–10) which relies heavily on Levinas' position on ethics and knowledge.)

If truth is primary, then the criteria of epistemology, cognition and knowledge take precedence over moral standards. The interests of knowledge predominate. Truth absorbs and transforms goodness for its own purposes. There is a long tradition of the self-absorption of knowledge (Aristotle, Hegel). Socrates requires us to pause and learn what right and wrong are before we act. Cain asks if he is his brother's keeper and is thus already condemned. Knowledge, even about morality, is insufficient, inadequate and inappropriate. Inasmuch as these terms themselves are products of knowledge, they too are insufficient. The position of knowledge, and general assumptions regarding knowledge, must once again be re-examined.

For knowledge to be knowledge it must turn upon itself, retrieve its project, deliberate, probe and prove it. Knowing must always decide beforehand what will count as knowledge. Even if there is a paradigm shift, the shift always makes sense in retrospect. Knowledge cannot be taken by surprise. Through its method it claims objectivity and the right to critique. Its decisions beforehand exclude the importance of ethics.

Ethics, on the other hand, does not satisfy knowledge: it disrupts knowledge. Ethics does not move on the level of knowledge, reason, themes or representation. It is not a movement towards or away from light. It is a trembling and hesitant movement that cannot be measured, towards the height and destitution of the other person. Its force is not that of the sufficiency of reasons, or of ideologies that abuse knowledge in its weak moments. In this way the access to an acritical approach is finally unlocked. Moral force cannot be reduced to cognitive cogency, acts of consciousness or decisions of the will. Ethical obligations lie in the refusal of concepts, in pre-thematic demands, social responses prior to and also beyond thematic thought. In other words, ethics disrupts the whole project of knowing with another call: responsibility. Goodness is better than and beyond the true and false. Knowledge cannot demand responsibility. As long as there is merely knowledge of underdevelopment, poverty, deprivation and nothing more, there will never be relief and change.

What is prior to the a priori conditions of cognition is the relationship with the alterity of the other person in an obligation to respond to that other person, a responsibility to and for the other person that comes from him but is mine. Movement towards the other must not be confused with the epistemological search for immediacy. Such immediacy has been shown to be contradictory. Knowledge of itself knows of no sufficient reason to set its sufficient reasons in motion. It only knows sufficient reasons; it knows nothing more compelling than reason.

Knowledge only wants more knowledge, wider and more firmly established knowledge, more comprehensive knowledge. All our expectations are fixed on more knowledge and, of course, more information (the 'critique' tradition). What is lacking in reason is its *raison d'etre*, its why. As long as this 'why' lacks meaning, a reminder of the famous paradox of Dupuy is in place: more and more information, but less and less meaning. The movement that sustains knowledge while remaining outside it is the ethical situation – there are others.

The ethical situation is excessive. The excess of the ethical claim is what contests knowledge and, as a non-epistemic contestation makes for the seriousness of the ethical situation. The ethical situation is a unique relation, without distance or union. Distance and unification are epistemic notions: objects and subjects. The proximity of the one to the other, the face-to-face relation, refuses to objectify, to discriminate, and resolves to honour, respond and care. The only thing it refuses is to be abused.

This constitutes the ethical relation. Its components are the alterity of the other, one's own passivity, the other's command and own responsibility. It should never be forgotten: the ethical situation is not a hiding place from responsibilities. Each one has to respond to the other instead of directing claims to the other's responsibility. In other words, in this unique relation no room is left for exploitation and parasitism – the firm ethical standpoint of Michel Serres.

Knowledge, however, is not degraded by these views. It is an important invention of the ethical situation and as such has tremendous ethical significance beyond its tendency to hide away its own origins. Knowledge emerges from the ethical situation because of exigencies within that situation itself. In this sense commitment to the other is more important and appropriate than critique of the other. Here we encounter an appeal to an acritical stance with which Michel Serres should assist.

### 9.3.4 The philosophy of Hermes (Michel Serres)

The most appropriate discussion in this regard is Serres' introduction to his book *La Communication* (1969), which is the first volume in a series of five with the general title *Hermès*. This introductory chapter gives an excellent overview of the most important arguments used by Serres to demonstrate the difference between a critical/dialectical and an acritical/network approach. The *Hermès* series together with other publications after this constitute Michel Serres' philosophy of information. According to him this philosophy accommodates communication as well as a philosophy of science with very clear ethical undertones.

Serres' acritical philosophy lives under quite different assumptions than those of the critique movement. Back to Latour (1987: 90–1): 'There is no centre and no substitution of one metalanguage that would overmaster all the others. The result of his commentary is a crossover, in the genetic sense, whereby characters of one language are crossed with attributes of another origin.' He then sums up Serres' position in the following words: '[F]or Michel Serres, the Critique has been a long parenthesis that is now put to a close [see the End of Criticism (Serres 1995)].' The task and the duties of the 'critique' philosopher are to reverse the pecking order, to reverse the force relations between masters. The 'critique' philosopher wants to bring religion to an end and make all disciplines, including philosophy, enter on the 'sure path of science'. The political overtone of this reversal of power relations was to at last emancipate the people and the mind from the tyranny of the senses, of beliefs, of the things, of the world' (Latour, 1987: 91).

What is our task in the information era against this background? When there is no belief in metalanguage, when history has not been divided up by revolutions, when mastery has not overmastered the world? What sort of enlightenment does one get when there is no critique? What emancipation is in store? What ethical implications are to be entertained? These questions are indeed explored by Serres' philosophy. In a recently published interview he explicitly emphasised how the chaotic, the fractal, the uncertain fascinate him, inspire his philosophical endeavours totally opposed to the solidity, certainty and fixity of the 'critique' tradition. Stupidity calls for stability (Serres, 2014: 85, 114).

From this brief overview of the four thinkers one thing should be clear: the ethical forms an integral part of the thought of each of them and cannot and should not be understood as a separate entity or discipline. The separation of the ethical from the thoughtful knowing activity is a matter of the 'critique' tradition. In acritical thinking the ethical is simply a matter of how and in what terms we think, namely always in terms of responsibility. Edgar Morin (2004: 13) can assist us here. 'Ethics manifests itself to us as a moral challenge. Its imperative is born from the essence of human individuality, namely the strenghtening of human spirituality with the injunction of an obligation.' But Morin (2004: 63−70) continues, in a chapter on the ethics of thought, with the claim that the bond between knowledge and obligation must be continuously confirmed − they belong together. 'The principle of intellectual consciousness is inseparable from the principle of moral consciousness.' For this reason the ethics of knowledge contains the struggle against the blindness and illusion of ignorance. The brief exploration of Serres' acritical style of thinking is based on this inseparable unity of the intellectual knowing consciousness and ethical moral consciousness.

What should be attended to is the relationship between an acritical philosophy per se and an acritical philosophy *of information*. The two belong together and will be dealt with in that sense. Some crucial moments in his style of thinking style will be highlighted with the explicit help, in some repsects, of Latour.


## 9.4   Acritical philosophy: a radically different mode of thinking

Some more specific characteristic points regarding the acritical position need to be highlighted. This thinking emerges from the depths of human beings and takes us beyond rationality and morality to the common roots of both of these. Kant's 'transcendental imagination' may be seen as a good example. It is a mode of thinking which is in line with 'the mode of information' explored by Mark Poster (1990) as well as Michel Serres' attitude as 'a marvellous reader' who sees 'reading as a journey'. In view of one of the most important facets of our discipline, a theme which becomes more important than ever before in the information era, namely reading, and in the spirit of this chapter the focus will be, first of all, on an acritical thinking about reading. In emphasising some core characteristics of the acritical position it may make sense to start with reading as the first core characteristic.

### 9.4.1   Acritical philosophy: acritical thinking about reading

Something to be considered here is a comparative study of the readings of Serres and Barthes of Balzac − *Hermaphrodite* (1987b) and *S/Z* (1974) respectively − that should be very interesting. For the moment, however, I wish to focus in a more general way on Serres as reader.

We must try to understand in what sense Serres is not a critique philosopher. For this purpose we have to take critique in the mundane sense of literary criticism for two reasons: firstly, for a large part of his career Serres published books which pertain to this genre. Secondly, every science, including the so-called hard *ones*, is defined by a certain *way* of practising a peculiar kind of exegesis. Here we rely once more on the well-formulated articulation of Latour (1987) on Serres as a 'marvellous reader'. 'Tell me how you comment on a writing or inscription, and I will tell you what kind of epistemology you hold on to. Understanding Serres' conception of commentary is also a *way* of understanding his conception of the sciences [and of knowledges]' (Latour, 1987: 86).

### The critique tradition of literary criticism and comment

The critic has a vocabulary, but so has the text under scrutiny.

1. There is a question or direction: which one does the interpretation? The critic of course, in terms of his/her metalanguage that makes sense of the infra-language of the text.
2. There is a question of size: the critic's vocabulary is enormously shorter than the text's repertoire. This is why the metalanguage is said to explain something. With two words in the critic's repertoire, for instance *Oedipus complex*, many novels or plays can be explained.
3. The question of precedence or of mastery: who dominates the other? The commentator: critics are much stronger than the texts they dominate and explain, establish and analyse. The mastery is so complete that texts, novels, plays, myths, etc. are buried beneath stronger, more powerful commentaries (see Latour, 1987: 86).

### Serres as example of a marvellous reader ... an acritical reader

His principle:

> *The text under scrutiny is always more rigorous, more lively, more modern, than the commentator and always provides a richer repertoire. Who turns around them? The commentator. Who overmasters him? The humble and outdated texts. He would rather appeal to the pure beauty of the text beyond the boring scholarship of the critique.*
>
> *(Latour, 1987: 86)*

In this case, the case of the critical reader:

1. There is no metalanguage.
2. It is impossible to distinguish the provider of an explanation, the commentary or the commented text.
3. There is no precedence and no mastery either.

What he does about the relation of the commentary to the text, and of the text to things, he also does to the relationship of texts to things and on the relations of the sciences to the world.

Here is no room for the violence that one detects in the critique tradition. Very recently Serres (2014: 32) once more stresses his emphatic resistance against violence in whatever form with the firm statement that it his conviction that 'power corrupts thought' and for that very reason he 'never runs after power'.

## Acritical information/knowledge usage

Knowledge use is the core issue of information science and information work or practice and can never be separated from reading. The route of criticism has proved to be only relatively successful and in many respects not at all. In this regard there are some significant passages in one of Serres' books, *Statues* (1987a), referring to the extremely problematic issue of knowledge application or utilisation, and which suggest an alternative route, hopefully with more success. Eventually it will be demonstrated that this suggested success is due to invention and the cultivation of inventiveness through which knowledge should always be remoulded and reshaped to respond to and comply with needs and requirements. Needs and requirements are never fixed in the sense that they can be addressed in recipe-like terms. Originality, creativity and inventiveness are called for.

Some more decisive characteristics flow from this approach to a special kind of reading.

### 9.4.2  Acritical philosophy: in praise of complexity and comprehensiveness

Compare Michel Serres' celebration of complexity in *Hermès: L'Interference* (1972: 19–65). Be careful of 'une ethique purgative du savoir'. This is when complexity is sacrificed for simplicity, and then power can easily take over (Serres, 1972: 220–2). Very recently Serres (2014: 100) emphasises that his utopia is 'the utopia of a new society that finally manages to escape from the evil of power'.

Complexity is clear from the movements in the network of links and interactions, from a field of forces in which subject and object undergo interchanges (Serres, 1987a: 21). Our lack of understanding must very often be related to this moving complexity. George Steiner's famous essay 'On Difficulty' (1978) and Edgar Morin's *Introduction à la pensée complexe* [*Introduction to Complex Thinking*] (1990) are more than sufficient supportive examples.

### 9.4.3 Acritical philosophy: a philosophy of invention

Invention is only possible within this context of links, networks and interactions. All that can be achieved otherwise is innovation, which is not the same. The one is closed, the other open.

But what is 'a philosophy of information?' Is there room for, or a place for, such an endeavour, similar to the generally accepted ideas of a philosophy of history, of religion, of law, of language, of politics, and others? And who must work it out and is it an activity which should be taken seriously and why?

These perspectives can fruitfully be developed in terms of Serres' thinking (and according to his approach to reading as a journey).

Why this focus on Michel Serres? There are various reasons: the influential character of his works and thinking, widely translated and discussed, and the inspiration behind the actor-network theory of a number of French and British sociologists; the uniqueness of his views on information, especially his unique paradigmatic claims (an acritical philosophy of information); the key position in which information is put in the field of knowledge and information work; the special interdisciplinary position taken by him in his thinking about information, education, the sciences and literature. All these insights have a very specific bearing on our theme and on our subject field.

The way in which he developed his views on communication shows a very heavy focus on information. The central place allocated to information in this and the subsequent titles of the *Hermès* series and other publications justifies in the very first place the notion or idea of a 'philosophy of information' rather than that of communication, albeit firmly the case that the intimate relationship between these two terms should be carefully explored. What should also be noted is that we encounter in this thinker a very unique and special, and for me exciting and useful, interpretation of these terms, the fecundity and fruitfulness of which we should not lose sight. As a matter of fact this fecundity is precisely the issue that forms the core and focus of this study.(It is only when we move beyond the critique of the 'critique' tradition that invention becomes a possibility.)

### 9.4.4 Acritical philosophy: virtual worlds, cyberspace and collective intelligence

These developments pose new adventurous possibilities for reading. From the previous paragraphs the following comprehensive hypothesis can be generated as formulated by Pierre Lévy:

> *It is both possible and desirable to construct technical, social, and semiotic means that will effectively incarnate and materialize collective intelligence ... When we speak of virtual worlds we specifically refer to vast digital networks, computer memories, interactive, multimodal interfaces, quick and nomadic, which individuals can easily appropriate. This implies a 'readerly' relationship to knowledge that will differ from that which exists today, the inauguration of an unmediated communications space, a profound renewal of human relations, both within the context of work and within political life, a reinvention of democracy – all possibilities that are embodied in the ideal of the collective intellect. (1997: 23)*

A critique approach may be totally out of place in this context. Lévy continues:

> *The collective intellect is a kind of corporation in which each shareholder supplies as capital his knowledge, experience, and his/her ability to learn and teach. The intelligent collective neither submits to nor limits individual intelligences, but on the contrary exalts them, fructifies and reinvigorates them. This transpersonal subject is not merely the sum of individual intelligences. Rather, it gives rise to a qualitatively different form of intelligence, which is added to personal intelligences, forming a kind of collective brain. (1997: 23–4)*

All of a sudden the notion of intelligent communities emerges which is the ultimate ethico-intelligible development/invention as a consequence of virtuality and cyberspace. (For more about this see Lévy, 1993, 1997, 1998.)

What is called for is a new relationship to knowledge and obviously to the notion of subjectivity. The text moulds the subject.

As an illustration and demonstration of the above the following self-evident expressions need exploration: the inverse cathedral (a change in the hierarchies of knowledge – no longer of transcendent origin); the breakdown of the ontological iron curtain (mind/matter dichotomy); heterogenesis as the creation of alterity (thinking inventing the other as the core of ethics). The implications of these views for ethics and for human subjectivity seem very obvious.

### 9.4.5 Acritical philosophy: reinventing subjectivity

Guattari emphasises clearly:

> *The issue which returns with insistence is the following: how do we reinvent social practices that would give back to humanity – if it ever had it – a sense of responsibility, not only for its own survival but equally for all life on the planet, for animal and vegetable species, likewise for incorporeal species such as music, the arts, cinema, the relation with time, love and compassion for others, the feeling of fusion at the heart of the cosmos? (1995: 135)*

This is nothing but a magnificent ethical statement.

In this regard the following themes spring to mind as of vital importance: transpersonal (collective) subjectivity; pragmatogonic subjectivity (primacy of the object); resingularised subjectivity (the subject as singularity); and the subject of alterity (the face of the 'other'). (See also Serres (2001) for a new and different perspective on what it means to be human related to changes in peasant, professional and corporeal existence under the impact of technical developments.).

In view of the above, Guattari (1995: 135) states: 'subjectivity is returning as leitmotif'. He writes further:

> *[Subjectivity] is not a natural given any more than water or air. How do we produce it, capture it, enrich it, and permanently reinvent it in a way that renders it compatible with Universes of mutant value? How do we work for its liberation,*

*that is, for its resingularisation? Psychoanalysis, institutional analysis, film, litera-*
*ture, poetry, innovative pedagogies, town planning, architecture – all the disci-*
*plines will have to combine their creativity to ward off the ordeals of barbarism,*
*the mental implosion and chaosmic spasms looming on the horizon, and transform*
*them into riches and unforeseen pleasures, the promises of which, for all that are*
*all too tangible. (1995: 135)*

In a sense it can be stated that the new developments bring forward a new vision and conception of humanity. By making these disciplines converge information science can play a role in the resingularisation and reinvention of the ethical subject. 'There is an alarming danger', according to Dupuy (1980: 17), 'that we should forget that our main wealth is in man, in the power to marvel and in the capacity to surprise'. In other words, our real wealth is neither in computers nor in information technology, but in human beings. In this regard no contribution is more significant than that of Gernot Wersig (1990, 1993), an information scientist in Berlin, when he writes about *the human focus* of information science, especially related to information technology developments. Together with Wersig, Rainer Kuhlen (2004) is making an equally substantial contribution to human subjectivity in his work on information ethics with its specific focus on information technology and knowledge ecology and a specific emphasis on the necessary presence of fully repsonsible subjects in this context.

# References

Barthes, R. (1974). *S/Z*. Toronto: Farrar, Straus & Giroux.
Cohen, R. A. (Ed.), (1986). *Face to face with Levinas* Albany, NY: SUNY Press.
Deleuze, G. (1983). *Nietzsche and philosophy*. London: Athlone Press.
Dretske, F. (1981). *Knowledge and the flow of information*. Oxford: Basil Blackwell.
Dupuy, J.-P. (1980). Myths of the informational society. In K. Woodward (Ed.), *The myths of information: Technology and post-industrial culture*. London: Routledge.
Dupuy, J.-P. (2013). *Science: A theology in spite of itself. The mark of the sacred*. Stanford, CA: Stanford University Press.
Guattari, F. (1995). *Chaosmosis: An ethico-aesthetic paradigm*. Bloomington, IN: Indiana University Press.
Kuhlen, R. (2004). *Informationsethik: Umgang mit Wissen und information in elektronischen Raumen*. Konstanz: UVK Verlagsgesellschaft.
Latour, B. (1987). The enlightenment without the critique: A word on Michel Serres' philosophy. In A. Phillips Griffiths (Ed.), *Contemporary French philosophy*. Cambridge: Cambridge University Press.
Latour, B. (1988). *The Pasteurization of France*, esp. 'Part 2: Irreductions'. Cambridge, MA: Harvard University Press.
Lévy, P. (1993). *Les technologies de l'intelligence: L' avenir de la pensée à l'ère informatique*. Paris: Seuil (Points).
Lévy, P. (1997). *Collective intelligence: Mankind's emerging world in cyberspace*. New York: Plenum Trade.
Lévy, P. (1998). *Becoming virtual: Reality in the digital age*. New York: Plenum Trade.

Lyotard, J.-F. (1984). *The postmodern condition: A report on knowledge*. Minneapolis, MN: University of Minnesota Press.

Morin, E. (1990). *Introduction à la pensée complexe*. Paris: ESF.

Morin, E. (2004). *La méthode 6: Éthique*. Paris: Seuil.

Poster, M. (1990). *The mode of information*. Cambridge: Polity Press.

Serres, M. (1969). *Hermès I: La communication*. Paris: Minuit.

Serres, M. (1972). *Hermès II: L'Interférence*. Paris: Minuit.

Serres, M. (1987a). *Statues*. Paris: François Bourin.

Serres, M. (1987b). *L'Hermaphrodite: Sarrasine sculpteur*. Paris: Flammarion.

Serres, M. (1995). *Conversations on science, culture and time* (with Bruno Latour). Ann Arbor, MI: University of Michigan Press.

Serres, M. (2001). *Hominescence*. Paris: Le Pommier.

Serres, M. (2014). *Pantopie: De Hermès à petite poucette*. Paris: Le Pommier.

Steiner, G. (1978). *On difficulty and other essays*. Oxford: Oxford University Press.

Wersig, G. (1990). The changing role of knowledge in an information society. In D. J. Foskett (Ed.), *The information environment: A world view*. New York: Elsevier Science.

Wersig, G. (1993). *Fokus Mensch: Bezugspunktepostmoderner Wissenschaft: Wissen, Kommunikation, Kultur*. Frankfurt am Main: Peter Lang.

# Index

Printed in the United States
By Bookmasters